Swift by Example

Create funky, impressive applications using Swift

Giordano Scalzo

BIRMINGHAM - MUMBAI

Swift by Example

First published: June 2015

Production reference: 1120615

Published by Packt Publishing Ltd.
Livery Place
35 Livery Street
Birmingham B3 2PB, UK.

ISBN 978-1-78528-470-0

www.packtpub.com

Credits

Author
Giordano Scalzo

Reviewers
Eugene Mozharovsky

Alexey Smirnov

Sumit Tiwari

Commissioning Editor
Nadeem N. Bagban

Acquisition Editors
Richard Brookes-Bland

Nikhil Karkal

Content Development Editor
Neeshma Ramakrishnan

Technical Editor
Faisal Siddiqui

Copy Editor
Vikrant Phadke

Project Coordinator
Shweta Birwatkar

Proofreader
Safis Editing

Indexer
Tejal Soni

Production Coordinator
Melwyn D'sa

Cover Work
Melwyn D'sa

About the Author

Giordano Scalzo is a developer with 20 years of programming experience since the days of the ZX Spectrum. He has worked using C++, Java, .NET, Ruby, Python, and a ton of other languages whose names he has forgotten.

After several years of backend development, over the past 5 years, he has developed extensively for iOS, releasing more than 20 apps—apps that he wrote for clients, enterprises, or himself.

Currently, Giordano is a contractor in London, where he delivers code for iOS through his company, Effective Code (`http://effectivecode.co.uk`), aiming at quality and reliability. In his spare time, when he is not crafting retro game clones for iOS, he writes his thoughts at `http://giordanoscalzo.com`.

I'd like to thank my better half, Valentina, who lovingly supports me in everything I do. Without you, none of this would have been possible.

And, thanks to Mattia and Luca for giving me lots of smiles and hugs when I needed them.

About the Reviewers

Eugene Mozharovsky began his journey in computer science in 2010 with a school course on programming in Pascal. Then he explored Java himself, and it was a whole new world of object-oriented programming, a full-featured API, and powerful client-server techniques for him. In 2013, he switched to Mac OS and discovered his true passion in developing applications for Apple mobile devices. In summer 2014, Eugene fell in love with Swift and iOS 8 beta. He is currently working on a handy social app for students. When he isn't writing code, he tries to systematize physics for his own understanding of how the universe works, or to train his parrots.

Alexey Smirnov works as a software engineer in a small start-up called iRONYUN (http://ironyun.com). In his spare time, he enjoys building iOS apps using Objective-C and Swift. He obtained his master's degree in computer science from Stony Brook University, USA.

Sumit Tiwari is an avid programmer and computer enthusiast who has been obsessed with efficiently instructing machines since his early years. He has several years of experience in low-level programming with C and C++, and substantial skills with Java, Python, Ruby, MATLAB, and Verilog, among others. Sumit holds a BE in electronics and telecommunications from the University of Mumbai, where he passed with distinction. He also has a master's degree in electrical engineering from the State University of New York at Stony Brook, where he graduated by coming top in his class. He is presently working as a hardware engineer in the gorgeous Silicon Valley. A self-proclaimed philomath, Sumit is always on the lookout for new technologies to learn.

> I would like to thank my family (ma, pa, bro, and Tejal) for always encouraging me to be at my best and for instilling in me the will and courage to follow my heart. I am, and will always remain, indebted to them for everything.

www.PacktPub.com

Support files, eBooks, discount offers, and more

For support files and downloads related to your book, please visit www.PacktPub.com.

Did you know that Packt offers eBook versions of every book published, with PDF and ePub files available? You can upgrade to the eBook version at www.PacktPub.com and, as a print book customer, you are entitled to a discount on the eBook copy. Get in touch with us at service@packtpub.com for more details.

At www.PacktPub.com, you can also read a collection of free technical articles, sign up for a range of free newsletters, and receive exclusive discounts and offers on Packt books and eBooks.

https://www2.packtpub.com/books/subscription/packtlib

Do you need instant solutions to your IT questions? PacktLib is Packt's online digital book library. Here, you can search, access, and read Packt's entire library of books.

Why subscribe?

- Fully searchable across every book published by Packt
- Copy-and-paste, print, and bookmark content
- On-demand and accessible via a Web browser

Free access for Packt account holders

If you have an account with Packt at www.PacktPub.com, you can use this to access PacktLib today and view nine entirely free books. Simply use your login credentials for immediate access.

Table of Contents

Preface

The introduction of Swift during the WWDC 2014 surprised the entire community of iOS developers, who were waiting for the new API brought by iOS 8 and not to be transformed into beginners.

Besides the surprise, most of them understood that this would be a great opportunity to create a new world of libraries, patterns, best practices, and so on. On the other hand, communities of programmers in different languages who were intimidated by the first (and rough) impact of Objective-C started getting attracted by Swift, which was less intimidating given its friendly syntax.

Whether you are part of the first or second group, *Swift by Example* will introduce the world of app development to you. Through simple step-by-step chapters, this book will teach you how to build both utility and game apps and, while building them, you'll learn the basics of Swift and iOS.

What this book covers

Chapter 1, *Welcome to the World of Swift*, introduces the Swift syntax and the most important features brought forth by the language. To show you how to build a project with Xcode, a simple app is created.

Chapter 2, *A Memory Game in Swift*, shows the creation of a complete game, with images and animations, without using any game framework and using only the fundamental iOS libraries.

Chapter 3, *A TodoList App in Swift*, teaches you how to create a real-world utility app, handling library dependencies with Cocoapods.

Chapter 4, *A Pretty Weather App*, shows you how to create a nice-looking app that retrieves data from third-party servers.

Chapter 5, Flappy Swift, covers SpriteKit, the 2D iOS game engine, and the creation of a clone of the famous game *Flappy Bird*.

Chapter 6, Polishing Flappy Swift, completes the game by adding Game Center support and various "added value" touches.

Chapter 7, Cube Runner, covers SceneKit and 3D programming by implementing a 3D endless runner game with a space theme.

Chapter 8, Completing Cube Runner, demonstrates the addition of final touches and Game Center support to the game.

What you need for this book

In order to get the most out of this book, there are a few essentials you will need:

- A Mac computer running OS X 10.10.3 or higher
- Basic knowledge of programming is helpful
- Xcode 6.3 or higher
- An iPhone 5s or higher (the last app uses CoreMotion, which doesn't work in the simulator)

Who this book is for

If you are a seasoned Objective-C programmer who wants to learn Swift, or if you are an enthusiastic developer without any prior experience in developing iOS apps, this book is for you.

Conventions

In this book, you will find a number of text styles that distinguish between different kinds of information. Here are some examples of these styles and an explanation of their meaning.

Code words in text, database table names, folder names, filenames, file extensions, pathnames, dummy URLs, user input, and Twitter handles are shown as follows: "We can include other contexts through the use of the `include` directive."

A block of code is set as follows:

```
let mainWindow = UIWindow(frame: UIScreen.mainScreen().bounds)
 mainWindow.backgroundColor = UIColor.whiteColor()
 mainWindow.rootViewController = navigatorViewController
 mainWindow.makeKeyAndVisible()
 window = mainWindow
 return true
```

When we wish to draw your attention to a particular part of a code block, the relevant lines or items are set in bold:

```
let mainWindow = UIWindow(frame: UIScreen.mainScreen().bounds)
 mainWindow.backgroundColor = UIColor.whiteColor()
 mainWindow.rootViewController = navigatorViewController
 mainWindow.makeKeyAndVisible()
 window = mainWindow
 return true
```

New terms and **important words** are shown in bold. Words that you see on the screen, for example, in menus or dialog boxes, appear in the text like this: "Clicking on the **Next** button moves you to the next screen."

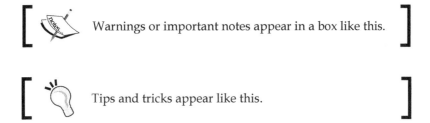

Warnings or important notes appear in a box like this.

Tips and tricks appear like this.

Reader feedback

Feedback from our readers is always welcome. Let us know what you think about this book—what you liked or disliked. Reader feedback is important for us as it helps us develop titles that you will really get the most out of.

To send us general feedback, simply e-mail feedback@packtpub.com, and mention the book's title in the subject of your message.

If there is a topic that you have expertise in and you are interested in either writing or contributing to a book, see our author guide at www.packtpub.com/authors.

Customer support

Now that you are the proud owner of a Packt book, we have a number of things to help you to get the most from your purchase.

Downloading the example code

You can download the example code files from your account at http://www. packtpub.com for all the Packt Publishing books you have purchased. If you purchased this book elsewhere, you can visit http://www.packtpub.com/support and register to have the files e-mailed directly to you.

Errata

Although we have taken every care to ensure the accuracy of our content, mistakes do happen. If you find a mistake in one of our books—maybe a mistake in the text or the code—we would be grateful if you could report this to us. By doing so, you can save other readers from frustration and help us improve subsequent versions of this book. If you find any errata, please report them by visiting http://www.packtpub. com/submit-errata, selecting your book, clicking on the **Errata Submission Form** link, and entering the details of your errata. Once your errata are verified, your submission will be accepted and the errata will be uploaded to our website or added to any list of existing errata under the Errata section of that title.

To view the previously submitted errata, go to https://www.packtpub.com/books/content/support and enter the name of the book in the search field. The required information will appear under the **Errata** section.

Piracy

Piracy of copyrighted material on the Internet is an ongoing problem across all media. At Packt, we take the protection of our copyright and licenses very seriously. If you come across any illegal copies of our works in any form on the Internet, please provide us with the location address or website name immediately so that we can pursue a remedy.

Please contact us at copyright@packtpub.com with a link to the suspected pirated material.

We appreciate your help in protecting our authors and our ability to bring you valuable content.

Questions

If you have a problem with any aspect of this book, you can contact us at
questions@packtpub.com, and we will do our best to address the problem.

1
Welcome to the World of Swift

Swift is a language so new that even most programming experts have barely a few months of experience in it. However, it borrows most of its features from several other programming languages, such as Ruby, Python Scala, Rust, Groovy, and even JavaScript and Haskell. So, anyone who approaches Swift will already feel at home, recognizing the patterns and features of their favorite programming languages.

Moreover, unlike Objective-C, whose learning curve is really steep for beginners, Swift is really friendly for newcomers, who can write code once they learn the basics of the language.

Nevertheless, mastering Swift when using its more advanced features, such as effectively integrating patterns of functional programming with object-oriented concepts, takes time, and most best practices still need to be discovered.

Also, Swift's language is just one part of the story. A lone language without an environment where it can build something is just a sterile exercise. Swift is not a general-purpose language, but a language with a specific goal—building apps for iOS and OS X using the Cocoa framework.

It's in this framework that the complexity resides; Cocoa is a very big framework, with thousands of APIs and different patterns and best practices. It has changed significantly over the course of its several releases, for example, moving from the delegate pattern to the use of blocks to make components interact with loose coupling.

More than knowing the language, the real challenge is in knowing the framework. I want to stress that the aim of this chapter is just to help you get the first grasp of what Swift's constructs look like, and not to be exhaustive, so expect to find a certain degree of simplification. Also, be aware that a deeper knowledge of the language can be achieved with books that specialize only in Swift learning, whereas the goal of this book is to teach you how to build apps using Swift.

The first look at Swift

The most obvious way to describe Swift is to compare it with Objective-C, which was the reference programming language for building Cocoa apps. Objective-C is an object-oriented programming language with similarities to dynamic languages, such as Ruby or Python. It is built on top of C, to which Apple has added features to make it modern, such as blocks, properties, and an **Automatic Reference Counter** (**ARC**) to manage the memory.

Swift is an object-oriented programming language with some functional programming characteristics. It aims to flatten the learning curve for the beginner, and to also provide more advanced features for the expert, adding more checks at runtime that could help make apps safer.

Objective-C is a loosely static-typed language; every variable must have a type, but it's possible to define a variable using the id type, reaching a sort of dynamic typing, where the type is evaluated at runtime. Thanks to its powerful runtime environment, it's possible to change the structure of a class—for example, add a method or variable—at runtime. This makes Objective-C a really flexible language, but it is also difficult to manage and prone to creating subtle bugs that are difficult to catch at runtime.

Swift is a strong static-typed language. This means that the type of a variable must be set and is evaluated at compile time. It also lacks any kind of metaprogramming at runtime, but this sternness, added to the functional patterns it supports, should help programmers eliminate an entire class of bugs, allowing apps to be more robust in a faster way.

However, the best way to learn a language is to play with it, and Xcode 6 has brought forth a really nice way to do it.

Let's go to the playground

Usually, the only way to experiment and learn a language until Xcode 5 was by creating a new app and writing code inside any method of that app. Then, you would compile and run it, reading the log or stopping using the debugger.

Xcode introduced the concept of a playground, which isn't an app or a program to be built, but a source file that is constantly compiled and evaluated every time it changes.

Xcode 6 can be downloaded for free from the Mac App Store at `www.appstore.com/mac/Xcode`. Once it is installed, go to **File | New | Playground**, as shown in this screenshot:

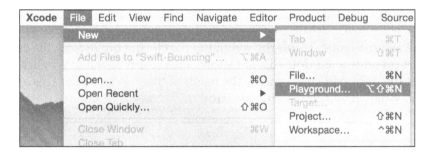

Without changing anything, you have created your first Swift program!
The following screenshot shows our first program:

```
// Playground - noun: a place where people can play

import Cocoa

var str = "Hello, playground"                    "Hello, playground"
```

The playground is split into two: to the left is our code, and to the right is the evaluation of the code on the left-hand side.

If we change the string from `"Hello, playground"` to `"Hello World!"`, as you can see in the following screenshot, the code is compiled and run without the need to select anything from the menu. This is because the compilation is triggered by the saving operation.

```
⬚    <   >   ⊞ HelloPlayground.playground

 1   //: Playground - noun: a place
           where people can play

 2

 3   import Cocoa

 4

 5   var str = "Hello, world"          "Hello, world"

 6
```

If we make an error, for example, by removing the closing quote from the string, the left part presents a red dot. This dot shows the error type when we click on it. Notice that the right part still presents the result of the previous run. This screenshot displays how the playground shows an error:

```
 1   // Playground - noun: a
           place where people
           can play

 2

 3   import Cocoa

 4

 5   var str = "Hello, world          Hello, world

 6   |             ⓘ Unterminated string literal
```

With the `println()` function, it is possible to print messages on a debug console, which can be opened by going to **View | Assistant Editor | Show Assistant Editor**, as shown in the following screenshot:

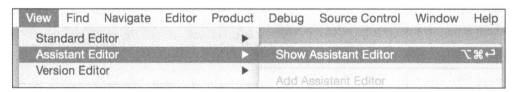

The console is basically another view inside the evaluation window, as you can see in this screenshot:

There is much more to learn about playground, but even with this much knowledge, we can dive into Swift without further ado.

The building blocks – variables and constants

As already said, Swift is a strong typed language, which means that every variable must be declared with the type it holds:

```
let name: String = "Paul"
let age: Int = 27
```

Using the `let` keyword, we define a constant—a variable that cannot change its value—and, as in math, the constant becomes the identity of the value itself. The following screenshot shows what the console looks like when we try to change the constant after we have defined it:

To define a variable, we can use the `var` keyword:

```
var name: String = "Paul"
var age: Int = 27
name = "John"
age = 29
```

We can change the value of a variable, paying attention to set a new value of the same kind. Otherwise, an error will be raised, as shown in this screenshot:

```
1  var name: String =
       "Paul"
2  var age: Int = 27
4  name = 29
5  |
```

```
x                        Console Output
Playground execution failed: /var/folders/hn/
bypbckdd1nnd73xzkjhxlsfc0000gn/T/lldb/46699/playground86.swift:
2:8: error: type 'String' does not conform to protocol
'IntegerLiteralConvertible'
name = 29
     ^
```

Speaking of type declaration, Swift is smarter than just requiring the type of a variable. If the value of the variable is set during its declaration, Swift can understand the type without the need for an explicit type. This feature is called type inference, and it allows us to create more concise code. For example, we can write code like the following:

```
let bassPlayer = "Paul"
let bassPlayerAge = 27
let guitarPlayer = "John"
let guitarPlayerAge = 29
```

Obviously, the type is mandatory if a variable is declared without being initialized:

```
var bassPlayer: String
var bassPlayerAge: Int
var guitarPlayer: String
var guitarPlayerAge: Int
```

Because it's really difficult to track all the changes made to a mutable variable, it is good practice to use constants as much as we can, and use variables only to contain the status in a small and well-defined scope in which it's easy to understand whether the code is correct or not.

Collect variables in containers

A variable is the minimum information that we can handle, but, sometimes, it is useful to group variables together. Swift provides three types of containers for this purpose: tuple, array, and dictionary.

A tuple is a limited set of heterogeneous values, like this, for example:

```
let bassPlayer = (name: "Paul", surname: "McCartney", age: 27)
```

In the declaration of a tuple, each piece of information is separated by a comma (,), each variable is a name-value pair separated by a colon (:), and all the elements are surrounded by a pair of parentheses.

To access the elements of a tuple, it is possible to use a dot notation, specifying the name of a variable:

```
bassPlayer.name    // Paul
bassPlayer.surname // McCartney
bassPlayer.age     // 27
```

A tuple can also be defined as an unnamed collection, that is, without specifying the names of the elements:

```
let bassPlayer = ("Paul", "McCartney", 27)
```

In this case, to access the elements, we must use their positions inside the tuple:

```
bassPlayer.0 // Paul
bassPlayer.1 // McCartney
bassPlayer.2 // 27
```

It is also possible to unwrap the values of a tuple and use them in simple external values, assigning each value inside the tuple to specific variables:

```
let bassPlayer = ("Paul", "McCartney", 27)
let (name, surname, age) = bassPlayer
println(name)
println(surname)
println(age)
```

An array is an unnamed list of homogeneous values:

```
var band = ["Paul", "John"]
```

An array has a number of elements. These elements can be asked for using the `count` property:

```
band.count // 2
```

Each element can be accessed using square brackets ([]) around the index of the value:

```
band[0] // Paul
band[1] // John
```

Just as in a tuple, the first index starts from 0.

Unlike Objective-C, where containers have mutable and immutable implementation, in Swift, it depends on the way in which the variable is declared — with `let` or with `var`.

If an array is mutable, we can change the value at a particular index, but we can also add elements using the `append` method:

```
band.append("George")
band.append("Ringo")
```

Moreover, using the sum operator (+), it is possible to create a new array that contains all the elements of the two previous arrays:

```
let theBeatles = band + ["George", "Ringo"]
```

The third container Swift provides is a dictionary, which is a sort of named-index array. Its syntax is similar to that of a tuple — using a name-value list separated by commas and surrounded by square brackets:

```
var band = ["bass": "Paul", "guitar": "John"]
```

Each value can be reached using the key inside the square brackets:

```
band["bass"]   // Optional("Paul")
band["guitar"] // Optional("John")
```

The value retrieved is not exactly the value we inserted during the initialization, but it is wrapped by an optional, which means that the result can be either a real value or `nil`. For example, if we use a key that is not present, the value returned is nil:

```
band["keyboard"] // nil
```

We'll see optionals later in this chapter. For the moment, it's enough to know that to extract the value from an optional, we must use the exclamation mark (!). Pay attention: you must do this only if you are sure that a value is inside an optional value. Otherwise, a runtime error will occur, as shown in this screenshot:

Controlling the flow

The most basic construct used to control the flow is the conditional check, which executes a piece of code if the condition provided is true:

```
var name = "Jim"
if name == "Paul" {
    println("Let's play the bass")
} else if name == "John" {
    println("Let's play the guitar")
} else if name == "George" {
    println("Let's play the sitar")
} else if name == "Ringo" {
    println("Let's play the drums")
} else {
    println("What do you want to play?")
}
```

The parentheses around the condition are optional, but the curly braces are required, even in the case of a single statement.

The `switch` block in Swift is more powerful than in other languages. It is a nicer way of writing a chain of `if` statements:

```
var name = "Jim"
switch name {
case "Paul":
    println("Let's play the bass")
case "John":
    println("Let's play the guitar")
case "George":
    println("Let's play the sitar")
case "Ringo":
    println("Let's play the drums")
default:
    println("What do you want to play?")
}
```

Whereas other languages' switch constructs handle-only integers, in Swift, we can have different types of conditional variables.

The list of possible values must be exhaustive, and, in this case, a `default` case must be provided.

A case block is executed until the entered variable's value matches the case. Swift is smart enough to break a case block on completion, so you don't have to explicitly break out of the switch at the end of case's code.

If you want the same behavior of case in Objective-C, which means continuing if there is no break command before the next case statement, you must add the fallthrough keyword, as shown here:

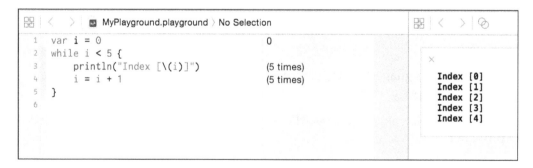

As said earlier, switches are more than this, but we'll see better when we implement the apps.

Until now, we have created only linear code, without jumping around or going back. It's now time to introduce the loop constructs provided by Swift. A loop is a statement that allows a block of code to be executed repeatedly, controlled by an exit condition.

The most basic kind is the while loop, where the loop is executed if a condition is true, as depicted in this screenshot:

```
1   var i = 0                          0
2   while i < 5 {
3       println("Index [\(i)]")        (5 times)
4       i = i + 1                      (5 times)
5   }
6
```

Index [0]
Index [1]
Index [2]
Index [3]
Index [4]

To illustrate the `while` loop, we introduce the string format, which is a handy way to insert a part of code to evaluate inside a string—using a backslash (\\) followed by parenthesis, (). The contained element is evaluated and the result replaces the expression. In other programming languages, this is called interpolation.

Another kind of loop is fast enumeration, which permits to iterate through an array without using an index, but by accessing the values straightaway, as shown in the following screenshot:

If we want to fast-enumerate through an array, and have also provided the index of the item, we can use the `enumerate` function. The following screenshot shows the use of enumerate, which basically returns an array of tuples containing the index and the value:

Transforming the values using functions

Swift is a multiparadigm language that mixes object-oriented programming with functional patterns.

The former organizes the code around objects, which are constructs with variables and functions in imperative way. This means telling the software how to execute the instructions one after the other. The latter defines the structures and elements of code as an evaluation of functions in a declarative way, which means defining *what the elements are* instead of *how the elements behave*.

These two paradigms—apparently opposite—give more flexibility to the developer, who can leverage one or the other, depending on the context.

In Swift, functions are first-class citizens, which means that they can be assigned to variables, or they can be passed as either parameters or return values of other functions.

A function in Swift is a named block of instructions that can be initialized, executed, passed as a parameter, or returned as a return value.

A function is declared using the `func` keyword and by enclosing the code to be executed around curly braces (`{}`):

```
func greet() {
    println("Hello, world!")
}
greet() // Hello, world!
```

In Swift, a function can be declared in anonymous way; in this case, it is called a **closure**:

```
let greet = {
    println("Hello, world!")
}
greet() // Hello, world!
```

A function can have a parameter, which is defined inside parentheses:

```
func greet(name: String) {
    println("Hello, \(name)!")
}
greet("Jim") // Hello, Jim!
```

When a function is defined as a closure, the parameters are inside the open curly brace and the `in` keyword separates them from the block of instructions:

```
let greet = { (name: String) in
    println("Hello, \(name)!")
}
greet("Jim") // Hello, Jim!
```

A function can return a value, which is defined using the arrow (`->`) in the declaration:

```
func greet(name: String) -> String {
    return "Hello, \(name)!"
}
println(greet("Jim")) // Hello, Jim!
```

In a consistent manner, the closure defines the return value after the parameters:

```
let greet = { (name: String) -> String in
    return "Hello, \(name)!"
}
println(greet("Jim")) // Hello, Jim!
```

A function can have more than one parameter:

```
func greet(name: String, greeting: String) -> String {
    return "\(greeting), \(name)!"
}
println(greet("Jim", "Hi")) // Hi, Jim!
```

As we can see from this example, the parameters during the call are passed in a positional way; this could be a source of confusion in certain functions where it isn't easy to understand or remember the role of the parameters:

```
func greeting(surname: String, firstname: String) -> String {
    return "My name is \(surname), \(firstname) \(surname)"
}

greeting("James", "Bond") //My name is James, Bond James
```

In this case, prepending the hash character (#) to the name of the parameter in the declaration of the function and labels during calls become mandatory:

```
func greeting(#surname: String, #firstname: String) -> String {
    return "My name is \(surname), \(firstname) \(surname)"
}

greeting(surname: "Bond", firstname: "James") //My name is James, Bond
James
```

It's important to note, as we'll see when we'll discuss classes, that when a function is defined in the context of a class, all the labels apart from the first are mandatory, without the need to add the hash character (the first label is optional for compatibility with Cocoa's naming convention, where the name of the method contains the label of the first).

Structs – custom compounds type

Earlier in this chapter, we saw how to group variables using tuples; starting from this concept, Swift offers a way to create complex custom types through **structs**.

A struct is a container of different elements, with the possibility to add functions to manipulate them.

Starting from the example we used for the tuple, we can define a struct in this way:

```
struct Player{
    let name: String
    let surname: String
    let age: Int
    let instrument: String
}

let bassPlayer = Player(name: "Paul", surname: "McCartney",
    age: 27,
    instrument: "bass")
let guitarPlayer = Player(name: "John", surname: "Lennon",
    age: 29,
    instrument: "guitar")
```

We can access the elements of a struct using the dot notation that we used for the named tuple:

```
guitarPlayer.name         // John
guitarPlayer.instrument // guitar
```

This form doesn't seem much different from a tuple, but the structs are more powerful than this.

For example, we can add a function inside the struct:

```
struct Player{
    let name: String
    let surname: String
    let age: Int
    let instrument: String
    func fullname() -> String{
        return "\(name) \(surname)"
    }
}
bassPlayer.fullname()  // Paul McCartney
```

One of the basic principles of functional programming is to have functions that deal only with immutable elements — they receive immutable objects and return immutable objects.

In this way, the mutable state is not shared in different places of the program, adding complexity to the code because a variable can be mutated in different places.

The `struct` construct was created with this principle in mind: to enforce immutability. When a struct variable is assigned to another variable, it is assigned by copy. This means that a new struct is created with the same values as the previous struct. The same happens when a struct is passed as a function argument. The nature of the struct is also known as the **ValueType**.

On the contrary, classes (which we'll see in the next section) are passed by reference. This means that only the address of the object is copied and the variable points to the same object.

As just mentioned, although it is better to have immutable structs, it's possible to define variables inside a struct, making it possible to change their values:

```
struct Player{
    var name: String
    var surname: String
    var age: Int
    var instrument: String
    func fullname() -> String{
        return "\(name) \(surname)"
    }
}

var guitarPlayer = Player(name: "John", surname: "Lennon",
    age: 29,
    instrument: "guitar")
guitarPlayer.fullname()              // John Lennon
guitarPlayer.name    = "Joe"
guitarPlayer.surname = "Satriani"
guitarPlayer.fullname()              // Joe Satriani
```

As already said, a struct is a container of elements; these elements are called properties. Other related properties can be created starting from already defined properties.

A struct in Swift offers the mechanism of computed properties to create related properties. These are basically functions disguised as properties:

```
struct Player{
    var name: String
    var surname: String
    var age: Int
    var instrument: String
    var fullname: String {
        return "\(name) \(surname)"
    }
```

```
    }

    var guitarPlayer = Player(name: "John", surname: "Lennon",
        age: 29,
        instrument: "guitar")

    println(guitarPlayer.fullname) //John Lennon
```

Note that from a caller point of view, a computed property is indistinguishable from a defined property, so it's also possible to define a way to change it:

```
    import Foundation

    struct Player{
        var name: String
        var surname: String
        var age: Int
        var instrument: String
        var fullname: String {
            get { return "\(name) \(surname)" }
            set(newFullname) {
              let names = newFullname.componentsSeparatedByString(" ")
              name = names[0]
              surname = names[1]
            }
        }
    }
    var guitarPlayer = Player(name: "John", surname: "Lennon",
        age: 29,
        instrument: "guitar")

    guitarPlayer.fullname = "Joe Satriani"
    println(guitarPlayer.name)      //Joe
    println(guitarPlayer.surname) //Satriani
```

There are a few things to talk about in this snippet.

First of all, we needed to use import Foundation to use the componentsSeparatedByString method, which creates an array of elements, splitting the string using the parameter string as a separator.

Inside the definition of the computed property, we defined two functions: a getter (get), which is the same code that we used in the previous example, and a setter (set), which accepts a string as parameter. In the function body, split the parameter in tokens, separated by an empty space, and assign the first value to name and the second to surname.

As already mentioned, a struct is a ValueType in Swift, such as an integer, a string, an array, and so on. This means that an instance of a struct is copied when assigned to a new variable or passed as a parameter:

```
struct Player{
    var name: String
    var surname: String
    var age: Int
    var instrument: String
}

var originalPlayer = Player(name: "John", surname: "Lennon",
    age: 29,
    instrument: "guitar")

var newPlayer = originalPlayer
newPlayer.name = "Joe"
newPlayer.surname = "Satriani"

originalPlayer.surname // Lennon
newPlayer.surname      // Satriani
```

A struct is also copied when it is passed a parameter in a function:

```
var originalPlayer = Player(name: "John", surname: "Lennon",
    age: 29,
    instrument: "guitar")

func transformPlayer(var player: Player) -> Player {
    player.name = "Joe"
    player.surname = "Satriani"
    return player
}

var newPlayer = transformPlayer(originalPlayer)

originalPlayer.surname // Lennon
newPlayer.surname      // Satriani
```

This knowledge of structs is enough to start using them efficiently.

Classes – common behavior objects

If you already know another object-oriented programming language, you might be wondering whether there are classes in Swift, and, if so, why we haven't them introduced earlier.

Of course there are! In the end, the main purpose of Swift is to create iOS or OS X apps using Cocoa, which is an object-oriented framework.

Nevertheless, with Swift being a multiparadigm programming language, classes are no longer the central concepts around which everything is built, as in object-oriented languages. However, they are a way to encapsulate the business logic.

Let's explore classes by altering the previous example to use classes instead of structs:

```
class Player{
    var name: String
    var surname: String
    var age: Int
    var instrument: String
    init(name: String, surname: String, age: Int, instrument: String){
        self.name = name
        self.surname = surname
        self.age = age
        self.instrument = instrument
    }
}

var originalPlayer = Player(name: "John", surname: "Lennon",
    age: 29,
    instrument: "guitar")
```

Basically, instead of the `struct` keyword, we used `class`, and we also needed to provide an initializer with all the parameters to initialize the instance (a constructor is a method called when the object is instantiated and initialized).

At first sight, it seems that class and struct are the same construct, but, in reality, the difference is substantial and relative to the nature of the two constructs.

The main difference is that an instance of a class is copied by reference. This means that the object isn't copied, but the reference of the object is copied, so when we change the new object, we are changing the original object as well.

Let's convert the example of the structs using a class:

```
var originalPlayer = Player(name: "John", surname: "Lennon",
    age: 29,
    instrument: "guitar")

func transformPlayer(var player: Player) -> Player {
    player.name = "Joe"
    player.surname = "Satriani"
    return player
}

var newPlayer = transformPlayer(originalPlayer)

originalPlayer.surname // Satriani
newPlayer.surname      // Satriani
```

We can see in the log of the playground that the function changed `originalPlayer` as well.

The other main difference is that a class supports inheritance. This means that we can created a specialized version of a class, which is still of the same category as the original class, but has more characteristics:

```
class Guitarist: Player{
    var guitarBrand: String
    init(name: String, surname: String, age: Int, guitarBrand: String)
{
        self.guitarBrand = guitarBrand
        super.init(name: name, surname: name, age: age, instrument:
"guitar")
    }
}

var alienGuitarist = Guitarist(name: "Joe", surname: "Satriani",
    age: 31,
    guitarBrand: "guitar")
```

So, a guitarist is basically a player with a guitar.

Note that in the constructor, we need to initialize all the variables of our level (in our case, just one), and then call the parent initializer using the `super` keyword to continue the chain of initialization.

To help understand when to use a struct or a class, it is often stated to favor the use of structs over classes. When an object represents something concrete (for example, a view or a button), we must use a class. When we need to represent properties or values that don't exist as concrete real things, such as `Coordinates` or `Rect`, we must use structs.

Loose coupling with protocols

A good way to tame the complexity of code is to separate *what* an object does from *how* it does it.

This is accomplished by defining the interface of an object, namely the properties and the methods of a class or a struct.

If the class or struct adheres to a protocol, it must implement all the methods defined in the protocol:

```
protocol Playable {
    func play()
}

class Player: Playable{

    //...

    func play() {
        // use instrument to play
    }
}
```

This allows us to call the defined methods without knowing the actual value of an instance:

```
func concert(band: [Playable]){
    for player in band {
        player.play()
    }
}
```

The concept of protocols is widely used in Cocoa for loose coupling and permitting an object to interact without knowing which kind of implementation it has.

Check the existence of an optionals value

We have already seen optionals when we discussed the dictionary.

The introduction of optionals is a radical, phenomenal change from Objective-C, where it is allowed to call a method on a nil object without crashing the app, and the method call is silently discarded.

It might be handy in several occasions, but it can often create really subtle, difficult-to-track, bugs. For example, if some objects of the UI are not connected to the controller and we try to change their values, we send messages to nil and nothing happens, leaving us without a clue as to what happened.

On the other hand, when we try to insert a nil object into a collection – array or dictionary – the app crashes at runtime.

Swift forces the developer to think of the nature of an element, whether it's always present or whether it could be nil.

An optional is declared using a question mark (?), and to make the code compile, the developer must check whether an optional value is `nil` before using it.

Also, an optional integer or optional string is not an ordinary integer or string; it's an integer or string wrapped in a container. To extract and evaluate the value inside the container, we must use the exclamation mark (!):

```
var optionalInt: Int?

if optionalInt != nil {
    let realInt = optionalInt!
    println("The value is [\(realInt)]")
} else {
    println("The value is nil!")
}
```

This pattern is so common that Swift allows us to create the unwrapped variable during the nil check:

```
var optionalInt: Int? = 3

if let realInt = optionalInt {
    println("The value is [\(realInt)]")
} else {
    println("The value is nil!")
}
```

As a good rule, it's recommended to use an optional as little as you can in your code, and to always check whether a variable is nil before using it.

Enumerations on steroids

Enumerations are common constructs in several programming languages, but in Swift, they are really powerful.

They are used when we have a limited and well-defined set of possible values, for example, the code responses for HTTP, or the suits of a card game.

While you can have only numeric-based enumerations in Objective-C, in Swift, enumerations can also be implemented with String:

```
enum Instrument: String {
    case Guitar = "guitar"
    case Bass = "bass"
    case Drums = "drums"
    case Sitar = "sitar"
    case Keyboard = "keyboard"
}
```

Using this enumeration, we can define a variable:

```
let instrument = Instrument.Drums
```

In this case, the constant infers the type from the initialization, but it is also possible to declare the type and using an abbreviated version of the value:

```
let instrument: Instrument = .Drums
```

Because the constant is an instrument, the compiler is expecting a value of the enumeration to assign to it, and it becomes superfluous when declaring the kind of enumerations on the right side.

We have already seen the `switch` construct, and it's really useful with enumeration, and in such a case, a statement contains a value of the enumeration:

```
let instrument: Instrument = .Drums

switch instrument {
case .Guitar:
    println("Let's play guitar")
case .Bass:
    println("Let's play bass")
case .Drums:
    println("Let's play drums")
case .Sitar:
    println("Let's play sitar")
case .Keyboard:
```

```
    println("Let's play keyboard")
}
// Let's play drums
```

As previously mentioned, the cases of a `switch` must be exhaustive, and all possible values must have a case; this enforces Swift to eliminate, as much as it can, the chances of introducing bugs because of distraction or superficiality. For every case, as in optionals, the developer is forced to pay attention and make a decision, which can be wrong of course, but at least it's not because he forgets to test a condition.

A really advanced feature of enumerations in Swift is the possibility to associate values with members. For example, we can add the number of strings for guitar and the brand for keyboard:

```
let keithEmersonInstrument: Instrument = .Keyboard("Hammond")
let steveVaiInstrument: Instrument = .Guitar(7)
let instrument = steveVaiInstrument

switch instrument {
case .Guitar(let numStrings):
    println("Let's play a \(numStrings) strings guitar")
case .Bass:
    println("Let's play bass")
case .Drums:
    println("Let's play drums")
case .Sitar:
    println("Let's play sitar")
case .Keyboard(let brand):
    println("Let's play a \(brand) keyboard")
}

// Let's play 7 strings guitar
```

Here, you can see that to extract the value from a value, we need to use the binding inside the case.

Enumerations are more powerful than what we have seen in this section, but this is enough to understand their power, which, when linked with the features of `switch` statements, make them one of most important additions to Swift.

A Guess the Number app in Swift

As mentioned in the introduction of this chapter, learning a language is just half of the difficulty in building an app; the other half is the framework. This means that learning a language is not enough. In this part of the chapter, we'll implement a simple *Guess the Number* app, just to become familiar with Xcode and part of the CocoaTouch framework.

The app is...

Our first complete Swift app is a *Guess the Number* app—a classic educational game for children where the player must guess a number generated randomly by the app.

For each guess, the app tells the player whether the guess is greater or lower than the generated number (also called the secret number).

Before diving into the code, we must define the interface of the app and the expected workflow.

This game presents only one screen, which is shown in the following screenshot:

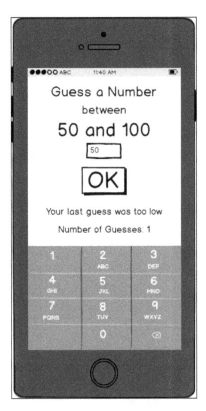

At the top of the screen, a label reports the name of the app—**Guess a Number**.

In the next row, another static label with the word **between**, connects the title with a dynamic label that reports the current range. The text inside the label must change every time a new number is inserted. A text field at the center of the screen is where the player will insert their guess.

A big button, with **OK** written on it, is the command that confirms that the player has inserted the chosen number.

The last two labels give feedback to the player:

- **Your last guess was too low** is displayed if the number inserted is lower than the secret number
- **Your last guess was too high** is displayed if it's greater than the secret number

The last label reports the current number of guesses. The workflow is straightforward:

1. The app selects a random number.
2. The player inserts their guess.
3. If the number is equal to the secret number, a popup tells the player that they have won, and shows them the number of guesses.
4. If the number is lower than the secret number but greater than the lower bound, it becomes the new lower bound. Otherwise, it is silently discarded.
5. If the number is greater and lower than the upper bound, it becomes the new upper bound. Otherwise, it's, again, silently discarded.

Building a skeleton app

Let's start building the app - select a new project by going to **File | New | Project...**, as shown in this screenshot:

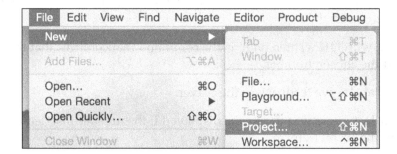

The following screenshot shows Xcode asking for the type of app to be created. The app is really simple, so we choose **Single View Application**:

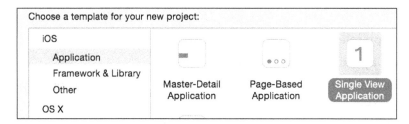

Before starting to write code, we need to complete the configuration by adding the organization identifier, using the reverse domain name notation, and **Product Name**. Together, they produce a **Bundle Identifier**, the unique identifier of the app.

Pay attention to the selected language, which must obviously be Swift. Here is a screenshot that shows you how to fill in the form:

Once done with this data, we are ready to run the app by going to **Product | Run**, as shown in this screenshot:

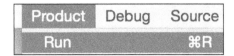

After the simulator finishes loading the app, we can see our magnificent creation—a shiny, brilliant white page!

We can stop the app by going to **Product | Stop**, as shown in the following screenshot:

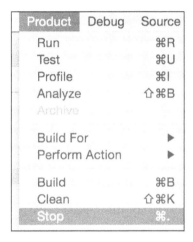

Now we are ready to implement the app.

Adding the graphic components

When we are developing an iOS app, it is good practice to implement the app outside-in, starting from the graphics.

By taking a look at the files generated by the Xcode template, we can identify the two files that we'll use to implement Guess the Number:

- `Main.storyboard`: This contains the graphics components
- `ViewController.swift`: This handles all of the business logic of the app

Here is a screenshot that presents the structure of the files in an Xcode project:

Let's start selecting the storyboard file to add the labels.

The first thing we notice is that the canvas is not the same size or ratio as an iPhone and an iPad. To handle different sizes and different devices, Apple (since iOS 5) added a constraints system, called AutoLayout, as a system to connect the graphics components in relative way, regardless of the actual size of the running device.

As Autolayout is beyond the scope of this chapter, we'll implement the created app only for iPhone 6.

After deciding our target device, we need to resize the canvas as per the real size of the device. From the tree structure at the right, we select **ViewController**, as shown here:

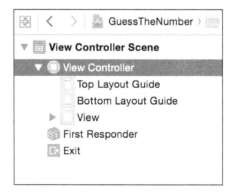

After having done that, we move to the right-hand side, where there are the properties of the ViewController. There, we select the tab containing **Simulated metrics**, in which we can insert the requested size. The following screenshot will help you locate the correct tab:

Now the size is the expected size, we can proceed to add labels, text fields, and the buttons from the list in the bottom-right corner of the screen.

To add a component, we must choose it from the list of components. Then, we must drag it onto the screen, where we can place it at the expected coordinates.

This screenshot shows the list of UI components, called an object library:

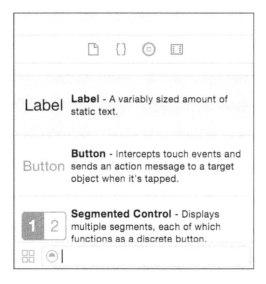

When you add the text field, pay attention to selecting **Number Pad** as the value for **Keyboard Type**, as illustrated in the following screenshot:

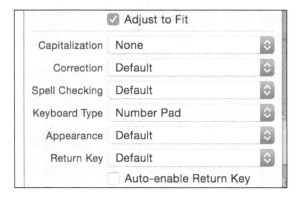

After selecting values for all the components, the app should appear as shown in the mockup we had drawn earlier, which this screenshot can confirm:

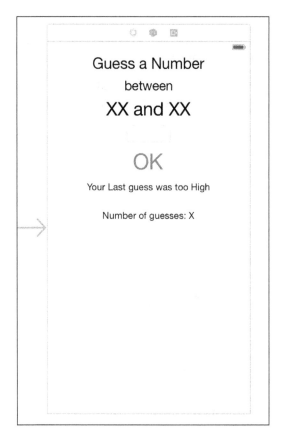

Connecting the dots

If we run the app, the screen is the same as the one in the storyboard, but if we try to insert a number into the text field and then press the button, nothing happens.

This is because the storyboard is still detached from the ViewController, which handles all of the logic.

To connect the labels to the ViewController, we need to create instances of a label prepended with the @IBOutlet keyword. Using this signature, Interface Builder — the graphic editor inside Xcode — can recognize the instances available for connection to the components:

```
class ViewController: UIViewController {
    @IBOutlet weak var rangeLbl: UILabel!
    @IBOutlet weak var numberTxtField: UITextField!
    @IBOutlet weak var messageLbl: UILabel!
    @IBOutlet weak var numGuessesLbl: UILabel!

    @IBAction func onOkPressed(sender: AnyObject) {
    }
}
```

We have also added a method with the @IBAction prefix, which will be called when the button is pressed.

Now, let's move on to Interface Builder to connect the labels and outlets.

First of all, we need to select **View Controller** from the tree of components, as shown in this screenshot:

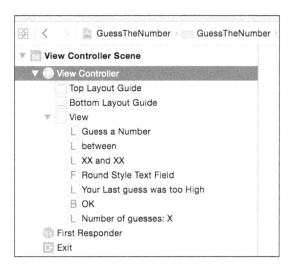

In the tabs to the right, select the outlet views, the last one with an arrow as a symbol. The following screenshot will help you find the correct symbol:

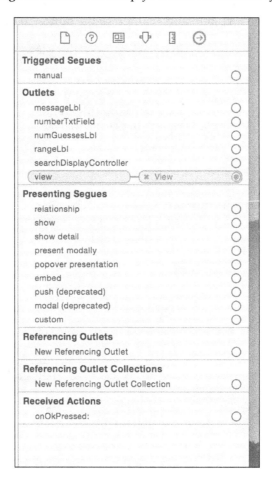

This shows all the possible outlets to which a component can be connected.

Upon moving the cursor onto the circle beside the **rangeLbl** label, we see that it changes to a cross. Now, we must click-and-drag a line to the label in the storyboard, as shown in this screenshot:

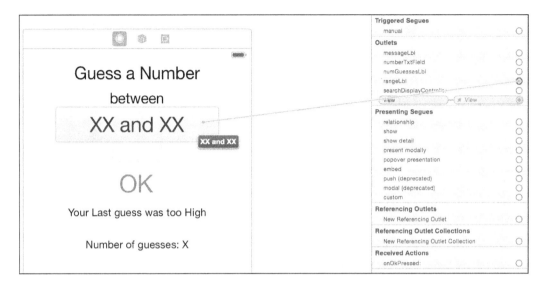

After doing the same for all the labels, the following screenshot shows the final configurations for the outlets:

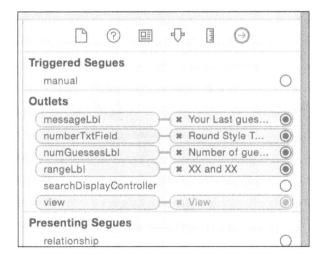

For the action of the button, the process is similar: select the circle close to the **onOkPressed** action, and drag a line to the **OK** button, as shown in this screenshot:

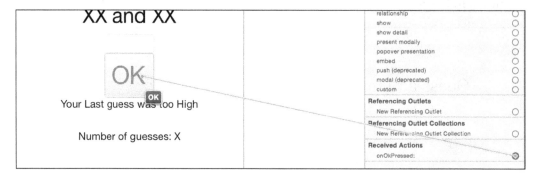

When the button is released, a popup appears, with the list of possible events to connect the action to.

In our case, we connect the action to the **Touch Up Inside** event, which is triggered when we release the button without moving from its area. The following screenshot presents the list of the events raised by the UIButton component:

Now, suppose we added a log command like this one:

```
@IBAction func onOkPressed(sender: AnyObject) {
    println(numberTxtField.text)
}
```

Then, we can see the value of the text field we insert printed on the debug console.

Now that all the components are connected to their respective outlets, we can add the simple code required to create the app.

Adding the code

First of all, we need to add a few instance variables to handle the state:

```
private var lowerBound = 0
private var upperBound = 100
private var numGuesses = 0
private var secretNumber = 0
```

Just for the sake of clarity, and the separation of responsibilities, we create two extensions to the ViewController. An extension in Swift is similar to a category in Objective-C—a distinct data structure that adds a method to the class it extends.

Because we don't need the source of the class that the extension extends, we can use this mechanism to add features to third-party classes, or even to CocoaTouch classes.

Given this original purpose, extensions can also be used to organize the code inside a source file. This could seem a bit unorthodox, but if it doesn't hurt and is useful, why not use it?

The first extension contains the logic of the game:

```
private extension ViewController{
    enum Comparison{
        case Smaller
        case Greater
        case Equals
    }

    func selectedNumber(number: Int){
}

    func compareNumber(number: Int, otherNumber: Int) -> Comparison {
}
}
```

Note that the `private` keyword is added to the extension, making the methods inside private. This means that other classes that hold a reference to an instance of ViewController can't call these private methods.

Also, this piece of code shows that it is possible to create enumerations inside a private extension.

The second extension is for rendering all the labels:

```
private extension ViewController{
    func extractSecretNumber() {
    }

    func renderRange() {
    }

    func renderNumGuesses() {
}
    func resetData() {
}
    func resetMsg() {
}
    func reset(){
        resetData()
        renderRange()
        renderNumGuesses()
        extractSecretNumber()
        resetMsg()
    }
}
```

Let's start from the beginning, which is the `viewDidLoad` method in the case of the ViewController:

```
override func viewDidLoad() {
    super.viewDidLoad()
numberTxtField.becomeFirstResponder()
    reset()
}
```

When the `becomeFirstResponder` method is called, the component called — `numberTxtField` in our case — gets the focus, and the keyboard appears.

After that, `reset()` is called:

```
func reset(){
    resetData()
    renderRange()
    renderNumGuesses()
    extractSecretNumber()
    resetMsg()
}
```

This basically calls the reset method of each component:

```
func resetData() {
    lowerBound = 0
    upperBound = 100
    numGuesses = 0
}

func resetMsg() {
    messageLbl.text = ""
}
```

Then, the method is called and is used to render the two dynamic labels:

```
func renderRange() {
    rangeLbl.text = "\(lowerBound) and \(upperBound)"
}

func renderNumGuesses() {
    numGuessesLbl.text = "Number of Guesses: \(numGuesses)"
}
```

It also extracts the secret number using the `arc4random_uniform` function, and performs some typecast magic to align to the expected numeric type:

```
func extractSecretNumber() {
    let diff = upperBound - lowerBound
    let randomNumber = Int(arc4random_uniform(UInt32(diff)))
    secretNumber = randomNumber + Int(lowerBound)
}
```

Now, all the action is in the `onOkPressed` action (pun intended):

```
@IBAction func onOkPressed(sender: AnyObject) {
    let number = numberTxtField.text.toInt()
if let number = number {
    selectedNumber(number)
} else {
 var alert = UIAlertController(title: nil,
             message: "Enter a number",
             preferredStyle: UIAlertControllerStyle.Alert)
  alert.addAction(UIAlertAction(title: "OK",
             style: UIAlertActionStyle.Default, handler: nil))
  self.presentViewController(alert,
                 animated: true,
                 completion: nil)
    }
    }
```

Here, we retrieve the inserted number. Then, if it is valid (that is, it's not empty, not a word, and so on), we call the `selectedNumber` method. Otherwise, we present a popup asking for a number.

All the juice is in `selectedNumber`, where there is a `switch` case:

```
func selectedNumber(number: Int){
        switch compareNumber(number, otherNumber: secretNumber){
//....
```

The `compareNumber` basically transforms a compare check into an `Enumeration`:

```
func compareNumber(number: Int, otherNumber: Int) -> Comparison{
        if number < otherNumber {
            return .Smaller
        } else if number > otherNumber {
            return .Greater
        }

        return .Equals
    }
```

Back to the `switch` statement of `selectedNumber` — it first checks whether the number inserted is the same as the secret number:

```
case .Equals:
var alert = UIAlertController(title: nil,
            message: "You won in \(numGuesses) guesses!",
            preferredStyle: UIAlertControllerStyle.Alert)
          alert.addAction(UIAlertAction(title: "OK",
            style: UIAlertActionStyle.Default,
            handler: { cmd in
              self.reset()
              self.numberTxtField.text = ""
            }))
          self.presentViewController(alert,
            animated: true, completion: nil)
```

If this is the case, a popup with the number of guesses is presented, and when it is dismissed, all of the data is cleaned and the game starts again.

If the number is smaller, we calculate the lower bound again, and then we render the feedback labels:

```
case .Smaller:
    lowerBound = max(lowerBound, number)
    messageLbl.text = "Your last guess was too low"
    numberTxtField.text = ""
    numGuesses++
    renderRange()
    renderNumGuesses()
```

If the number is greater, the code is similar, but instead of the lower bound, we calculate the upper bound:

```
case .Greater:
    upperBound = min(upperBound, number)
    messageLbl.text = "Your last guess was too high"
    numberTxtField.text = ""
    numGuesses++
    renderRange()
    renderNumGuesses()
}
```

Et voilà! With this simple code, we have implemented our app.

 You can download the code of the app from `https://github.com/gscalzo/GuessTheNumber`.

Summary

This was a really dense chapter because we squeezed in content, that usually needs at least a book to explain properly, in only tens of pages.

We took a quick look at Swift and its capabilities, starting from the definitions of variables and constants, and then how to define the control flow. After that, we moved on to structs and classes, seeing how they are similar in some ways, but profoundly different as philosophies. Finally, we created a simple game app, showing all the required steps in great detail.

Of course, simply after reading this chapter, nobody can be considered an expert in Swift and Xcode. However, the information here is enough to let you understand all of the code we'll be using in the upcoming chapters to build several kinds of apps.

In the next chapter, we'll continue to explore Swift and iOS by implementing another game—a memory game that will let us make use of the power of structs. You will also learn about some new things in UIKit.

A Memory Game in Swift

2

After learning the fundamental parts of the language, and getting a basic introduction to creating a simple app with Xcode, it's now time to build something more complex, but by using the basics from the previous chapter. This chapter aims to show you how to structure an app, creating clean and simple code, and how to make it appealing to the user with nice colors and smooth animations.

Compared to the previous chapter, this chapter is more advanced because I think the best way to learn new concepts is to see them in a real app. One of the many ways to show content in an iOS app is by using `UICollectionView`, which is a component that lays the subcomponents as a flow of cell. A good introduction to UICollectionView can be found at `http://nshipster.com/uicollectionview/`.

The app is...

The app we are going to implement is a UIKit implementation of a memory game—a solitaire version. A memory game, also known as *Concentration*, is a card game where the player must match all the cards, which start reversed, turning up two of them in each turn. If the cards match, they are removed from the table. Otherwise, they are turned down again and the score increases. The goal is to clear the table with the lowest score possible.

In our implementation, we are going to use only standard UIKit components, and to see another way of creating the interface in Xcode, we'll create all of our UI directly in code without using Interface Builder.

Let's start prototyping the screens. Despite this being an educational app, we want it to be a pretty and fun app, so we need at least one option to decide the difficulty, selecting the quantity of cards laid on the table.

The following are the screens we'll implement for the app; the first is for selecting the difficulty — basically selecting the number of the cards in the deck:

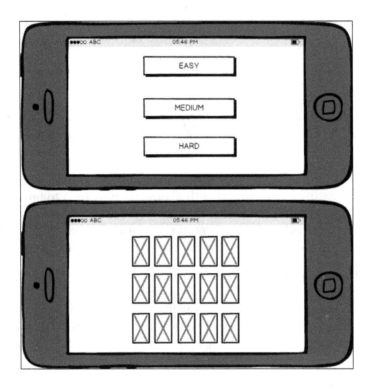

Building the skeleton of the app

As we have already seen in the previous chapter, we can create our app by going to **File | New | Project,** and then selecting **Single View Application** from the list of templates.

For simplifying the handling of different resolutions, our memory game is in landscape mode only, so when the creation of the template has been completed, uncheck **Portrait** as the allowed device orientation, as shown in the following screenshot:

The menu screen

Let's start implementing the first view, in which we can select the level of the game.

Implementing the basic menu screen

As we have planned to implement all of the UI in the code itself, we won't bother to touch the storyboard. We will proceed to open the `ViewController` class to implement the menu screen.

Looking at the mockup, we can see that we have three levels of difficulty: easy, medium, and hard. There are three buttons, each one used to select one of them. Also, the buttons are horizontally centered and vertically equidistant.

First of all, we define an enumeration to describe the difficulty.

Then, we implement the setup for the layout:

```
enum Difficulty {
    case Easy, Medium, Hard
}
```

Just for the sake of readability, we group the methods needed to implement a feature in a separated extension, leaving in the main class only the public functions and the variable definition. Although extensions were born for a different goal, which is to extend classes we don't have the source for, I've found that grouping together methods in an extension helps describe the goals of those methods. Matt Thompson, the creator of AFNetworking, the most used network library for iOS, used the same approach in Alamofire (`https://github.com/Alamofire/Alamofire`):

```
class ViewController: UIViewController {
    override func viewDidLoad() {
        super.viewDidLoad()
        setup()
    }
}

private extension ViewController {
    func setup() {
        view.backgroundColor = UIColor.whiteColor()

        buildButtonWithCenter(CGPoint(x: view.center.x,
            y: view.center.y/2.0),
            title: "EASY", color: UIColor.greenColor(), action:
"onEasyTapped:")
```

```
        buildButtonWithCenter(CGPoint(x: view.center.x,
            y: view.center.y),
            title: "MEDIUM", color: UIColor.yellowColor(), action:
    "onMediumTapped:")
        buildButtonWithCenter(CGPoint(x: view.center.x,
            y: view.center.y*3.0/2.0),
            title: "HARD", color: UIColor.redColor(), action:
    "onHardTapped:")
    }

    func buildButtonWithCenter(center: CGPoint,
    title: String, color: UIColor, action: Selector) {
        //...
    }
}
```

Again, we are not yet relying on AutoLayout to establish relations between the components, so we pass the coordinates of each button to the initializer method. In the same method, we also pass the text to be presented as a caption and the background color.

The last parameter, called action, contains the name of the method inside the ViewController that the button must call when pressed. The following implementation of buildButtonCenter() shows you how to create a button programmatically:

```
    func buildButtonWithCenter(center: CGPoint, title: String, color:
    UIColor, action: Selector) {
        let button = UIButton()
        button.setTitle(title, forState: .Normal)
       button.setTitleColor(UIColor.blackColor(),
                        forState: .Normal)

        button.frame = CGRect(origin: CGPoint(x: 0, y: 0), size:
    CGSize(width: 200, height: 50))
        button.center = center
        button.backgroundColor = color

        button.addTarget(self, action: action, forControlEvents:
    UIControlEvents.TouchUpInside)
        view.addSubview(button)
    }
```

The last statement before adding the button to the view is the way to connect a callback to an event - the programmatic equivalent of creating a line connecting an event of the button to @IBAction using Interface Builder. This is a technique we saw in the previous chapter.

Because all the actions are logically tied together, we create another extension to group them:

```
extension ViewController {
    func onEasyTapped(sender: UIButton) {
        newGameDifficulty(.Easy)
    }

    func onMediumTapped(sender: UIButton) {
        newGameDifficulty(.Medium)
    }

    func onHardTapped(sender: UIButton) {
        newGameDifficulty(.Hard)
    }

    func newGameDifficulty(difficulty: Difficulty) {
        switch difficulty {
        case .Easy:
            println("Easy")
        case .Medium:
            println("Medium")
        case .Hard:
            println("Hard")
        }
    }
}
```

If we run the app now by going to **Product | Run**, we can see that we have almost implemented the screen in the mockup, as you can see in the following screenshot:

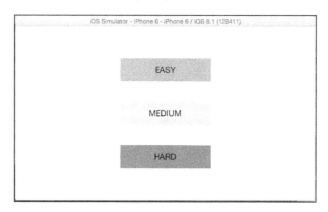

Also, by tapping the buttons, we can verify that the button calls the correct function. We must see the correct message in the console when we press a button.

Although the screen is how we expected to implement it, it isn't very appealing, so before proceeding to implement the game ViewController, we customize the color palette to make the UI prettier.

Creating a nice menu screen

Because the flat design is very fashionable lately, we go to `http://flatuicolors.com` to choose a few colors to decorate our components.

After choosing the color, we extend the `UIColor` class:

```
extension UIColor {
    class func greenSea() -> UIColor {
        return UIColor.colorComponents((22, 160, 133))
    }
    class func emerald() -> UIColor {
        return UIColor.colorComponents((46, 204, 113))
    }
    class func sunflower() -> UIColor {
        return UIColor.colorComponents((241, 196, 15))
    }
    class func alizarin() -> UIColor {
        return UIColor.colorComponents((231, 76, 60))
    }
}

private extension UIColor {
    class func colorComponents(components: (CGFloat, CGFloat,
CGFloat)) -> UIColor {
        return UIColor(red: components.0/255, green: components.1/255,
blue: components.2/255, alpha: 1)
    }
}
```

With this extended palette, we can change the setup of the ViewController:

```
func setup() {
    view.backgroundColor = UIColor.greenSea()

    buildButtonCenter(CGPoint(x: view.center.x, y: view.
center.y/2.0),
        title: "EASY", color: UIColor.emerald(), action:
"onEasyTapped:")
```

```
        buildButtonCenter(CGPoint(x: view.center.x, y: view.center.y),
              title: "MEDIUM", color: UIColor.sunflower(), action:
    "onMediumTapped:")
        buildButtonCenter(CGPoint(x: view.center.x, y: view.
    center.y*3.0/2.0),
              title: "HARD", color: UIColor.alizarin(), action:
    "onHardTapped:")
    }
```

The result, as shown in this screenshot, is definitely prettier, reminding us of a real card table:

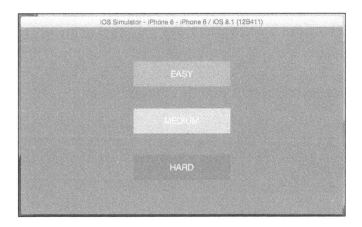

Now we can implement a proper newGame() function:

```
    func newGameDifficulty(difficulty: Difficulty) {
        let gameViewController = MemoryViewController(difficulty:
    difficulty)
        presentViewController(gameViewController, animated: true,
    completion: nil)
    }
```

 You can find the code at https://github.com/gscalzo/Memory/tree/menu.

The game screen

Before implementing the game, let's proceed to build the layout of the cards on the table.

The structure

After creating the `MemoryViewController` file, we add the class life cycle functions:

```swift
class MemoryViewController: UIViewController {
    private let difficulty: Difficulty

    init(difficulty: Difficulty) {
        self.difficulty = difficulty
        super.init(nibName: nil, bundle: nil)
    }

    required init(coder aDecoder: NSCoder) {
        fatalError("init(coder:) has not been implemented")
    }

    deinit{
        println("deinit")
    }

    override func viewDidLoad() {
        super.viewDidLoad()
        setup()
    }
}
// MARK: Setup
private extension MemoryViewController {
    func setup() {
        view.backgroundColor = UIColor.greenSea()
    }
}
```

Besides the initializer that accepts the chosen difficulty, although it's not used, we need to add the *required initializer* with `NSCoder`. Moreover, you should note that we need to call the parent initializer with `nibName` and the bundle, used when a UIViewController is built from an XIB file. If we called a plain `super.init()`, we would receive a runtime error, because the empty one is a *convenience initializer* — an initializer that calls a *required initializer* in the same class, which in our case is not implemented.

Although not mandatory, we have implemented the deinitializer as well, inserting just a debug log statement to verify that the class is correctly removed from the memory when dismissed. Thus, a retain cycle is avoided.

Finally, we come to this comment:

```swift
// MARK: Setup
```

This is a special comment that tells Xcode to present the sentence in the structure of a class, as shown in the following screenshot, to facilitate navigation to a different part of the class:

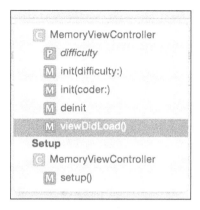

Adding the collectionView class

Let's move on to implementing the layout of the card. We'll use the UICollectionView class to lay the cards on the table. The UICollectionView class is a view that arranges the contained cells to follow a layout we set during the setup. In this case, we set a flow layout in which each card follows the previous one, and it creates a new row when the right border is reached.

We set the properties for the view and a model to fulfill the collection view:

```
private var collectionView: UICollectionView!
private var deck: Array<Int>!
```

Next, we write the function calls to set up everything in viewDidLoad, so that the functions are called when the view is loaded:

```
override func viewDidLoad() {
    super.viewDidLoad()
    setup()
    start()
}
```

The setup() function basically creates and configures CollectionView:

```
// MARK: Setup
private extension MemoryViewController {
    func setup() {
        view.backgroundColor = UIColor.greenSea()
```

```
        let space: CGFloat = 5

        let (covWidth, covHeight) = collectionViewSizeDifficulty(diffi
culty, space: space)
        let layout = layoutCardSize(cardSizeDifficulty(difficulty,
space: space), space: space)

        collectionView = UICollectionView(frame:
            CGRect(x: 0, y: 0, width: covWidth, height: covHeight),
            collectionViewLayout: layout)
        collectionView.center = view.center
        collectionView.dataSource = self
        collectionView.delegate = self
        collectionView.scrollEnabled = false
        collectionView.registerClass(UICollectionViewCell.self,
            forCellWithReuseIdentifier: "cardCell")
        collectionView.backgroundColor = UIColor.clearColor()

        self.view.addSubview(collectionView)
    }
```

After setting the color of the table, we define a constant, space, to set the space between every two cards.

Next, we calculate the size of the collection view given the difficulty, and, hence, the number of rows and columns; then, the layout. Finally, we put everything together to build the collection view:

```
    func collectionViewSizeDifficulty(difficulty: Difficulty, space:
CGFloat) -> (CGFloat, CGFloat) {
        let (columns, rows) = sizeDifficulty(difficulty)
        let (cardWidth, cardHeight) = cardSizeDifficulty(difficulty,
space: space)

        let covWidth = columns*(cardWidth + 2*space)
        let covHeight = rows*(cardHeight + space)
        return (covWidth, covHeight)
    }
```

The cardSizeDifficulty() function calculates the size of the collection view by multiplying the size of each card by the number of rows or columns:

```
    func cardSizeDifficulty(difficulty: Difficulty, space: CGFloat) ->
(CGFloat, CGFloat) {
        let ratio: CGFloat = 1.452
```

```
let (columns, rows) = sizeDifficulty(difficulty)
let cardHeight: CGFloat = view.frame.height/rows - 2*space
let cardWidth: CGFloat = cardHeight/ratio
return (cardWidth, cardHeight)
}
```

Sizing the components

As mentioned at the start of this chapter, we are not using AutoLayout, but we need to handle the issue of different screen sizes somehow. Hence, using basic math, we adapt the size of each card to the available size in the screen:

```
func layoutCardSize(cardSize: (cardWidth: CGFloat, cardHeight:
CGFloat), space: CGFloat) -> UICollectionViewLayout {
    let layout: UICollectionViewFlowLayout =
UICollectionViewFlowLayout()
    layout.sectionInset = UIEdgeInsets(top: space, left: space,
bottom: space, right: space)
    layout.itemSize = CGSize(width: cardSize.cardWidth, height:
cardSize.cardHeight)
    layout.minimumLineSpacing = space
    return layout
}
```

As mentioned before, the `UICollectionView` class shows a series of cells in its content view, but the way in which the cells are presented — as a grid or a vertical pile, the space between them — is defined by an instance of `UICollectionViewFlowLayout`.

Finally, we set up the layout, defining the size of each cell and how they are separated and laid out.

We have seen that there is a connection between the difficulty setting and the size of the grid of the cards, and this relation is simply implemented using `switch` statements:

```
// MARK: Difficulty
private extension MemoryViewController {
    func sizeDifficulty(difficulty: Difficulty) -> (CGFloat, CGFloat)
{
        switch difficulty {
        case .Easy:
            return (4,3)
        case .Medium:
            return (6,4)
        case .Hard:
```

```
            return (8,4)
        }
    }

    func numCardsNeededDifficulty(difficulty: Difficulty) -> Int {
        let (columns, rows) = sizeDifficulty(difficulty)
        return Int(columns * rows)
    }
}
```

Connecting the datasource and the delegate

You have probably noticed that when we created `CollectionView`, we set the ViewController itself as `dataSource` and `delegate`:

```
collectionView.dataSource = self
collectionView.delegate = self
```

A common pattern found in Cocoa in many components is the delegate pattern, where part of the behavior is delegated to another object, and that object must implement a particular protocol.

In the case of `UICollectionView`, and likewise for `UITableView`, we have to delegate one to provide the content for the view, the datasource, and the other to react to events from the view itself. In this way, the presentation level is completely decoupled from the data and the business logic, which reside in two specialized objects.

So, we need to implement the required methods of the protocols:

```
// MARK: UICollectionViewDataSource
extension MemoryViewController: UICollectionViewDataSource {
    func collectionView(collectionView: UICollectionView,
        numberOfItemsInSection section: Int) -> Int {
        return deck.count
    }

    func collectionView(collectionView: UICollectionView,
        cellForItemAtIndexPath indexPath: NSIndexPath) ->
UICollectionViewCell {
        var cell = collectionView.dequeueReusableCellWithReuseIdentifi
er("cardCell",
            forIndexPath: indexPath) as! UICollectionViewCell

        cell.backgroundColor = UIColor.sunflower()
        return cell
    }
}
```

As you can notice, in the method called for the cell at a certain position, we are calling a method to reuse a cell, instead of creating a new one. This is a nifty feature of `UICollectionView` that saves all the cells in a cache and can reuse those outside the visible view. This not only saves a lot of memory, but is also really efficient, because creating new cells during scrolling could be CPU-consuming and affect performance.

Because we want to see just the flow of the card, we use the default empty cell as the view cell, changing the color of the background:

```
// MARK: UICollectionViewDelegate
extension MemoryViewController: UICollectionViewDelegate {
    func collectionView(collectionView: UICollectionView,
didSelectItemAtIndexPath indexPath: NSIndexPath) {
    }
}
```

For the delegate, we simply prepare ourselves to handle a touch on the card. Because we don't need a real deck of cards, an array of integers is enough as a model:

```
    override func viewDidLoad() {
        super.viewDidLoad()
        setup()
        start()
    }

    private func start() {
        deck = Array<Int>(count: numCardsNeededDifficulty(difficulty),
repeatedValue: 1)
        collectionView.reloadData()
    }
```

Upon running the app now and choosing a level, we will have all our empty cards laid out, like this:

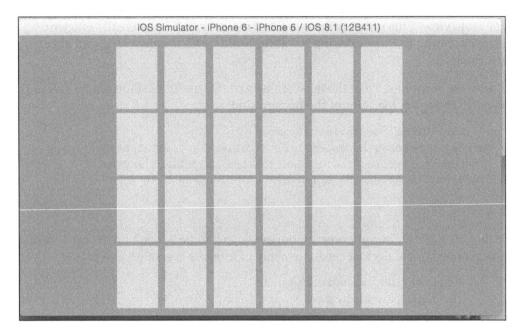

Using a different simulator and the iPhone 5 or 4S, we can see that our table adapts its size smoothly.

The code for the app implemented so far can be downloaded from https://github.com/gscalzo/Memory/tree/card_layout.

Implementing a deck of cards

So far, we have implemented a pretty generic app that lays out views inside a bigger view. Let's proceed to implement the foundation of the game—a deck of cards.

What we are expecting

Before implementing the classes for a deck of cards, we must define the behavior we are expecting, whereby we implement the calls in `MemoryViewController`, assuming that the `Deck` object already exists. First of all, we change the type in the definition of the property:

```
private var deck: Deck!
```

Then, we change the implementation of the `start()` function:

```
private func start() {
    deck = createDeck(numCardsNeededDifficulty(difficulty))
    collectionView.reloadData()
}

private func createDeck(numCards: Int) -> Deck {
    let fullDeck = Deck.full().shuffled()
    let halfDeck = fullDeck.deckOfNumberOfCards(numCards/2)
    return (halfDeck + halfDeck).shuffled()
}
```

We are saying that we want a deck to be able to return a shuffled version of itself, and which can return a deck of a selected numbers of its cards. Also, it can be created using the plus operator (+) to join two decks. This is a lot of information, but it should help you learn a lot regarding structs.

The Card entity

There isn't anything regarding the entities inside `Deck` so far, but we can assume that it is a `Card` struct, and that it uses plain enumerations. A `Suit` and a `Rank` parameter define a card, so we can write this code:

```
enum Suit: Printable {
    case Spades, Hearts, Diamonds, Clubs
    var description: String {
        switch self {
        case .Spades:
            return "spades"
        case .Hearts:
            return "hearts"
        case .Diamonds:
            return "diamonds"
        case .Clubs:
            return "clubs"
        }
    }
}


enum Rank: Int, Printable {
    case Ace = 1
    case Two, Three, Four, Five, Six, Seven, Eight, Nine, Ten
    case Jack, Queen, King
```

```
        var description: String {
            switch self {
            case .Ace:
                return "ace"
            case .Jack:
                return "jack"
            case .Queen:
                return "queen"
            case .King:
                return "king"
            default:
                return String(self.rawValue)
            }
        }
    }
}
```

Note that we have used an integer as a type in `Rank`, but not in `Suit`. That's because we want the possibility to create a `Rank` from an integer — its raw value — but not for `Suit`. This will soon become clearer.

We have implemented the `Printable` protocol in order to be able to print the enumeration. The `Card` parameter is nothing more than a pair of `Rank` and `Suit`:

```
struct Card: Printable, Equatable {
    private let rank: Rank
    private let suit: Suit

    var description: String {
        return "\(rank.description)_of_\(suit.description)"
    }
}
func ==(card1: Card, card2: Card) -> Bool {
    return card1.rank == card2.rank && card1.suit == card2.suit
}
```

Also, for `Card`, we have implemented the `Printable` Protocol, basically joining the description of its `Rank` and `Suit`. We have also implemented the `Equatable` protocol to be able to check whether two cards are of the same value.

Crafting the deck

Now we can implement the constructor of a full deck, iterating through all the values of the `Rank` and `Suit` enumerations:

```
struct Deck {
    private var cards = [Card]()
```

```
static func full() -> Deck {
    var deck = Deck()
    for i in Rank.Ace.rawValue...Rank.King.rawValue {
        for suit in [Suit.Spades, .Hearts,
                        .Clubs, .Diamonds] {
            let card = Card(rank: Rank(rawValue: i)!,
                suit: suit)

            deck.cards.append(card)
        }
    }
    return deck
}
}
```

Shuffling the deck

The next function we will implement is `shuffled()`:

```
// Fisher-Yates (fast and uniform) shuffle
func shuffled() -> Deck {
    var list = cards
    for i in 0..<(list.count - 1) {
        let j = Int(arc4random_uniform(UInt32(list.count - i))) +
i

        swap(&list[i], &list[j])
    }
    return Deck(cards: list)
}
```

The usual way to shuffle a deck of cards in a computer program is to use the **Fisher-Yates algorithm**. Starting from the first card, we iterate until the very end, each turn swapping the current card with a random card in the set with index greater than the current one. A complete explanation of this can be found on Wikipedia at `http://en.wikipedia.org/wiki/Fisher-Yates_shuffle`.

If you look carefully at the `swap()` function, you will see an ampersand (`&`) symbol before the parameters. It means that the parameters are `inout`, and that they can be changed inside functions. We can consider `inout` parameters as shared variables between the caller and the called.

Finishing the deck

We are almost done with the expected behavior of `Deck`; we just need to add the creation of a subset of `Deck`:

```
func deckOfNumberOfCards(num: Int) -> Deck {

    return Deck(cards: Array(cards[0..<num]))
}
```

Note that by using the notation for the range [..<], the upper bound is not included in the range, whereas by using [..], the upper bound is included. We can create that by exploiting the splicing feature of the Swift `Array`. Using the same trick, we create the sum operator:

```
func +(deck1: Deck, deck2: Deck) -> Deck {
    return Deck(cards: deck1.cards + deck2.cards)
}
```

The last function left is the `count` property, which we implement by using a computed property:

```
var count: Int {
    get {
        return cards.count
    }
}
```

Before moving on to implement the remainder of the game, we want to check whether everything works fine, so we add a log after creating the deck, like this:

```
deck = createDeck(numCardsNeededDifficulty(difficulty))
for i in 0..<deck.count {
    println("The card at index [\(i)] is [\(deck[i].description)]")
}
```

Unfortunately, the compiler complains that it doesn't know how to retrieve the element at a specified index.

For the purpose of mimicking the accessor of an array, Swift provides a special computed property to add to the definition of our struct— `subscript`. Implementing the subscript just involves forwarding the request to the `private` property cards:

```
subscript(index: Int) -> Card {
    get {
        return cards[index]
    }
}
```

Now the app compiles. If we run it, we get a console output like this:

```
The card at index [0]  is [8_of_clubs]
The card at index [1]  is [ace_of_spades]
The card at index [2]  is [ace_of_clubs]
The card at index [3]  is [ace_of_hearts]
The card at index [4]  is [9_of_hearts]
The card at index [5]  is [ace_of_hearts]
The card at index [6]  is [queen_of_clubs]
The card at index [7]  is [ace_of_clubs]
The card at index [8]  is [ace_of_spades]
The card at index [9]  is [queen_of_clubs]
The card at index [10] is [9_of_hearts]
The card at index [11] is [8_of_clubs]
```

 The source code for this block can be downloaded from `https://github.com/gscalzo/Memory/tree/foundation_for_cards`.

Put the cards on the table

Finally, let's add the card images and implement the entire game.

Adding the assets

Now that everything works, let's create a nice UI again.

First of all, let's import all the assets into the project. There are plenty of free cards assets on the Internet, but if you are lazy, I've prepared for you a complete deck of images ready for this game, and you can download them from `https://github.com/gscalzo/Memory/blob/master/Assets/CardImages.zip?raw=true`.

The archive contains an image for the back of the cards, and all the front images for the others. To include them in the app, select the image assets file from the project structure view, as shown in this screenshot:

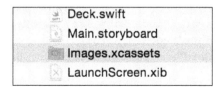

After selecting the catalogue, the images can be dragged into Xcode, as in the following screenshot:

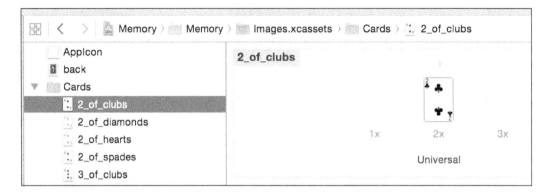

In this operation, you must pay attention and ensure that you move all the images from **1x** to **2x**. Otherwise, when you run the app, you will see them pixelate.

The CardCell structure

Let's go ahead and implement our CardCell. Again, we pretend that we already have the class, so we register that class during the setup of CollectionView:

```
func setup() {
    //...
    collectionView.registerClass(CardCell.self,
        forCellWithReuseIdentifier: "cardCell")
    //...
}
```

Then, we implement the rendering of the class when the datasource protocol asks for a cell, given an index:

```
func collectionView(collectionView: UICollectionView,
    cellForItemAtIndexPath indexPath: NSIndexPath) ->
UICollectionViewCell {
    var cell = collectionView.dequeueReusableCellWithReuseIdentifi
er("cardCell",
        forIndexPath: indexPath) as! CardCell
    let card = deck[indexPath.row]
    cell.renderCardName(card.description, backImageName: "back")
    return cell
}
```

We are trying to push as much presentation code as we can into the new class to decouple the responsibilities between `Cell` and the controller, which holds the model. `CardCell` contains only `UIImageView` to present the card images, and two properties to hold the names of the front and back images:

```
class CardCell: UICollectionViewCell {
    private let frontImageView: UIImageView!
    private var cardImageName: String!
    private var backImageName: String!

    override init(frame: CGRect) {
       frontImageView = UIImageView(frame: CGRect(x: 0, y: 0,
            width: frame.size.width,
            height: frame.size.height))
      super.init(frame: frame)
      contentView.addSubview(frontImageView)
      contentView.backgroundColor = UIColor.clearColor()
    }

    required init(coder aDecoder: NSCoder) {
        fatalError("init(coder:) has not been implemented")
    }

    func renderCardName(cardImageName: String, backImageName: String){
        self.cardImageName = cardImageName
        self.backImageName = backImageName
        frontImageView.image = UIImage(named: self.backImageName)
    }
  }
}
```

If you run the app now, you should see some nice cards face down.

Handling touches

Now, let's get them face up!

```
func collectionView(collectionView: UICollectionView,
    didSelectItemAtIndexPath indexPath: NSIndexPath) {
    let cell = collectionView.cellForItemAtIndexPath(indexPath)
        as CardCell
    cell.upturn()
}
```

This code is pretty clear, and now we only need to implement the upturn() function inside CardCell:

```
func upturn() {
    UIView.transitionWithView(contentView,
        duration: 1,
        options: .TransitionFlipFromRight,
        animations: {
            self.frontImageView.image =
                UIImage(named: self.cardImageName)
        },
        completion: nil)
}
```

By leveraging a handy function inside the UIView class, we have created a nice transition from the back image to the front image, simulating the flip of a card.

To complete the functions required to manage the card from a visual point of view, we implement the downturn() function in a similar way:

```
func downturn() {
    UIView.transitionWithView(contentView,
        duration: 1,
        options: .TransitionFlipFromLeft,
        animations: {
            self.frontImageView.image =
                UIImage(named: self.backImageName)
        },
        completion: nil)
}
```

To test them, we turn down the card 2 seconds after we turned it up. To run a delayed function, we use the dispatch_after function, but to remove the boilerplate call, we wrap it in a smaller common function:

```
extension UIViewController {
    func execAfter(delay: Double, block: () -> Void) {
        dispatch_after(
            dispatch_time(
                DISPATCH_TIME_NOW,
                Int64(delay * Double(NSEC_PER_SEC))
            ),
            dispatch_get_main_queue(), block)
    }
}
```

So, after having the card turned up, we turn it down using this newly implemented function:

```
func collectionView(collectionView: UICollectionView,
    didSelectItemAtIndexPath indexPath: NSIndexPath) {
        //...
        cell.upturn()
        execAfter(2) {
            cell.downturn()
        }
}
```

By running the app, we now see the cards turning up and down, with smooth and nice animation.

Finishing the game

In this section, we will finally be able to play the game.

Implementing the game logic

After having all the required functions in place, it's now straightforward to complete the game. First of all, we add the instance variables to hold the number of the pairs already made, the current score, and the list of selected cards turned up:

```
private var selectedIndexes = Array<NSIndexPath>()
private var numberOfPairs = 0
private var score = 0
```

Then, we put the logic when a card is selected:

```
func collectionView(collectionView: UICollectionView,
    didSelectItemAtIndexPath indexPath: NSIndexPath) {
    if selectedIndexes.count == 2 ||
        contains(selectedIndexes, indexPath) {
        return
    }
    selectedIndexes.append(indexPath)

    let cell = collectionView.cellForItemAtIndexPath(indexPath)
        as CardCell
    cell.upturn()

    if selectedIndexes.count < 2 {
        return
```

```
        }

        let card1 = deck[selectedIndexes[0].row]
        let card2 = deck[selectedIndexes[1].row]

        if card1 == card2 {
            numberOfPairs++
            checkIfFinished()
            removeCards()
        } else {
            score++
            turnCardsFaceDown()
        }
    }
```

We first check whether we have touched an already turned-up card or if we have two cards turned up. If not, we save the index. Then, we check whether we have flipped the first card, and, if not, we proceed to check the values of the cards.

The pattern of checking a condition and leaving the current function if the condition is `true` is called **Guard**. It helps make the code more readable by avoiding the use of the `else` clause and the nesting of curly braces.

We got a pair

As in the previous part of the source, we implement the missing actions in a private extension:

```
// MARK: Actions
private extension MemoryViewController {
    func checkIfFinished(){
    }
    func removeCards(){
    }
    func turnCardsFaceDown(){
    }
}
```

The first one checks whether we have completed all the pairs, and if so, it presents a popup with the score and returns to the main menu:

```
func checkIfFinished(){
    if numberOfPairs == deck.count/2 {
        showFinalPopUp()
    }
```

```
    }
    func showFinalPopUp() {
        var alert = UIAlertController(title: "Great!",
            message: "You won with score: \(score)!",
            preferredStyle: UIAlertControllerStyle.Alert)
        alert.addAction(UIAlertAction(title: "Ok", style: .Default,
handler: { action in
            self.dismissViewControllerAnimated(true, completion: nil)
            return
        }))

        self.presentViewController(alert, animated: true, completion:
nil)
    }
```

Note that in iOS 8, `UIAlertController` is slightly different from that in the previous version. In our case, a simple dialog box with an **Ok** button is enough.

If the cards are equal, we need to remove them:

```
        func removeCards(){
        execAfter(1.0) {
            self.removeCardsAtPlaces(self.selectedIndexes)
            self.selectedIndexes = Array<NSIndexPath>()
        }
    }

    func removeCardsAtPlaces(places: Array<NSIndexPath>){
        for index in selectedIndexes {
            let cardCell = collectionView.
cellForItemAtIndexPath(index)
                as CardCell
            cardCell.remove()
        }
    }
```

The `remove()` function in `CardCell` is similar to `turnUp()` and `turnDown()`, but instead of making a transition, it just performs an animation before hiding the cell:

```
func remove() {
    UIView.animateWithDuration(1,
        animations: {
            self.alpha = 0
        },
        completion: { completed in
            self.hidden = true
        })
    }
```

We played a wrong turn

Finally, if the cards are different, we need to turn them down:

```
func turnCardsFaceDown(){
    execAfter(2.0) {
        self.downturnCardsAtPlaces(self.selectedIndexes)
        self.selectedIndexes = Array<NSIndexPath>()
    }
}

func downturnCardsAtPlaces(places: Array<NSIndexPath>){
    for index in selectedIndexes {
        let cardCell = collectionView.
cellForItemAtIndexPath(index)
            as CardCell
        cardCell.downturn()
    }
}
```

Et voilà! The game is completed

As you can see in the following screenshot, the game presents smooth animation and nice images:

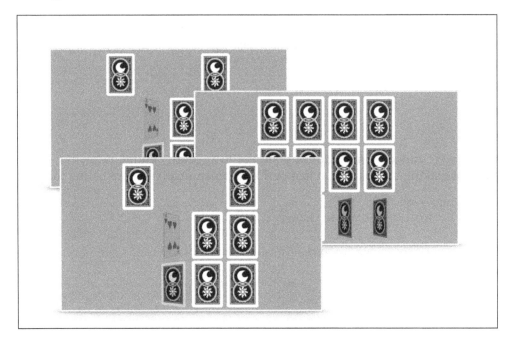

The complete source can be downloaded from `https://github.com/gscalzo/Memory`.

Summary

In this chapter, we implemented our first complete app, beginning with using basic components, and then moving on to use more advanced techniques to create smooth animation, without relying on game frameworks such as Cocos2d or SpriteKit.

We saw when, and how, to use structs in an effective way, and how to split responsibilities among different classes. Moreover, we experimented and saw how to separate different parts of the same class using extensions, and how to design an interface of a class or struct, pretending we have already implemented it.

You have learned a few things about puzzle games, and it's now time to move on to something different, but more similar to a normal app we'll have a chance to work on—a *TodoList* app.

3
A TodoList App in Swift

After playing in the first two chapters, it's now time to move on to something different—exploring how to implement a utility app and solving the most common problems you face during the development of an iOS app.

This will be a really dense chapter, because we'll cover several problems, such as AutoLayout, interactions between ViewControllers, using third-party libraries without getting mad, configuring the project, and handling library dependencies.

The app is…

The most common, and perhaps the simplest, way to learn to develop an iOS app is by starting with a to-do list where the user can add tasks, show them, and change their status.

You need to be aware that a generic utility app for iOS must handle the following:

- Getting data from the user
- Presenting data obtained from the user
- Manipulating data
- Somehow saving data
- Synchronizing data with a server

Our *Todolist* app has all of these features except the last one, and it can be considered the prototype of all utility apps. Let's define the specifications of our app. The first, and the most useful, screen must present the list of Todos, as this screenshot shows:

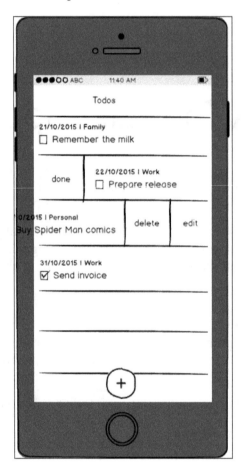

Each one out of the list of Todos has a description, due date, and containing list (Family, Personal, Work, and so on), which can be used to filter and catalogue the tasks. A checkbox indicates whether the corresponding task is done or still open.

The user can perform three different actions: edit, delete, or set a particular Todo task as done. The action buttons are normally hidden, but the user can see them by sliding the Todo cell either to the right or to the left.

A single button, centered at the bottom, allows, the creation of a new `Todo` task. When this button is pressed, a new view slides in from the right, with a back button in the top-left corner to allow you to go back to the main view. This is a common UI pattern, used when screens are related in a sort of master-detail relationship.

The following screenshot shows the screen where the user can create a `Todo` task:

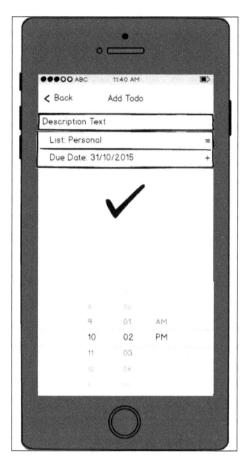

The user can add a description using `TextField`. They can define the containing list and the due date by selecting their buttons. However, both the fields have default values: **Personal** for the former, and the date (the day after tomorrow), for the due date.

When the **Due Date** button is selected, the keyboard slides down, and a time picker allows the user to select the due date. When the **List** button is selected, a new controller appears. When the user is satisfied with the content, they can press the checkmark button to save the `Todo` task and to go back to the main controller.

As we have seen in the previous screenshot, the user can edit the Todo task. This operation is similar to the creation of the Todo task, so it makes sense to use the same screen. In it, instead of getting the default values, all the fields will be prepopulated with the values of the Todo task to edit.

As mentioned earlier, by pressing the **List** button, the screen changes to a new one, allowing us to select a list or create a new list, as shown in this screenshot:

Building a skeleton app

Let's start implementing the base structure on top of which we'll implement the entire app.

Implementing an empty app

Let's start creating a new app called *Todolist* using the **Single View Application** Xcode template. The app will be in portrait mode only, so you must uncheck **Landscape** from the allowed device orientations.

Although Apple has improved Interface Builder in Xcode 6, most developers still favor writing the layout in code instead of using Interface Builder. The common reasons, are that, with Interface Builder, it is more difficult to create reusable views, which makes work in a team difficult because of merging of the storyboard files; and in general, it is more difficult to debug a complex layout.

The main reason I prefer layout in code is that it is much easier to have everything under control if I use code. I can group the layout into functions, change the order of the constraints, add variables to them, and so on.

Although this may seem more verbose than creating constraints with a few clicks on Interface Builder, it is a technique that pays in the long term.

However, what works for me might not work for you, and because the layout of the following apps will be implemented by code, I recommend that you create the same layout using Interface Builder to get all the elements required to make an informed choice.

In this app, we are going to use AutoLayout directly in code, without using Interface Builder, so we can remove the storyboard from our project.

First of all, we must delete the `Main.storyboard` and `ViewController.swift` files. Then, from the general tab settings, we remove the entry for **Main Interface**, as shown in the following screenshot:

If you run the app now, you will see a black screen. This is because the SDK doesn't know which ViewController it needs to call. Let's create an empty ViewController, calling it `TodosViewController`. Then we add this code to the `AppDelegate` class:

```
func application(application: UIApplication,
        didFinishLaunchingWithOptions launchOptions:
        [NSObject: AnyObject]?) -> Bool {
  let viewController = TodosViewController()
  let navigatorViewController = UINavigationController(rootViewControll
er: viewController)

  let mainWindow = UIWindow(frame: UIScreen.mainScreen().bounds)
  mainWindow.backgroundColor = UIColor.whiteColor()
```

```
mainWindow.rootViewController = navigatorViewController
mainWindow.makeKeyAndVisible()
window = mainWindow
return true
}
```

This code instantiates this main ViewController. Then it puts it as the root ViewController inside `UINavigationController`, which is finally set up as the root ViewController of the app.

The `UINavigationController` is the base class for one of the most widely used types of navigation in iOS, where each new view is pushed on top of the current view, appearing from the right. When the new screen is dismissed, that is popped from the stack of the views, it disappears by sliding to the right.

If you run the app now, an empty screen with a navigation bar appears. Before moving on, we add the assets to the app. Despite the fact that we are using quite a few icons in *Todolist*, I provide the app icon and the add button only. In this book, we are planning to use a third-party library that provides icons in font format, without the need to insert images.

 The assets can be downloaded from `https://github.com/gscalzo/Todolist/raw/master/Assets/images.zip`.

Adding third-party libraries with CocoaPods

Before starting to implement the app, I want to introduce the secret weapon of productive iOS developers—CocoaPods.

CocoaPods (`http://cocoapods.org`) is the dependency manager for Cocoa projects that allows you to add a thousand libraries to your project by adding just one line of code to a configuration file. To add CocoaPods using Ruby, which is installed by default, you can type the following command in a terminal:

```
sudo gem install cocoapods
```

Then, we need to create the Podfile, where we will add the needed libraries. Consider this command:

```
pod init
```

It creates an empty Podfile, preconfigured to match our targets. We can now add the libraries to the Podfile:

```
target 'Todolist' do
   pod 'FontAwesomeKit',
        :git => "https://github.com/gscalzo/FontAwesomeKit.git"
   pod 'LatoFont',
        :git => "https://github.com/gscalzo/LatoFont.git"
   pod 'Cartography', '~> 0.1'
   pod 'MGSwipeTableCell', '~> 1.3.5'
end
```

You will see that you can select either the version of the library or the git path. This is really convenient when you need to modify a library to match your needs but you can't wait for the maintainer to merge the pull request and publish the new version. Now run the `install` command:

pod install

The libraries are downloaded and added as frameworks to your project without the need to touch any of the project settings—neat, isn't it?

> Pay attention to this: sometimes, Xcode doesn't like the fact that an external app changes a project while it is open in Xcode. So, before running the pod, you must close Xcode.

As the `pod` command says at the end of the installation, we should now use `Todolist.xcworkspace` instead of `Todolist.xcodeproj`.

By opening the workspace, we can see that we now have a **Pods** project, with all the libraries as subdirectories, as shown in the following screenshot:

Implementing the Todos ViewController

We want to separate different responsibilities into different classes, so we are going to implement two classes: `TodosViewController` to handle the UI and the commands received from the user, and `TodosDatastore` to handle the creation and changes in the entities.

These classes manipulate two entities: `Todo` and `List`. As already experimented, we implement these classes in a top-down fashion, starting from the ViewController, which basically presents just a button and a table view:

```
class TodosViewController: UIViewController {
    private let tableView = UITableView()
    private let addButton = UIButton()

    override func viewDidLoad() {
        super.viewDidLoad()

        setup()
        layoutView()
        style()
    }
}
```

Trying to reduce the public code as much as we can, in the main class, we leave only the `viewDidLoad()` function and the call to the three functions that we need to set up the controller:

```
// MARK: Setup
private extension TodosViewController{
    func setup(){
        title = "Todos"
        view.backgroundColor = UIColor.grayColor()
        tableView.registerClass(UITableViewCell.classForCoder(),
            forCellReuseIdentifier: "Cell")
        tableView.dataSource = self
        tableView.rowHeight = 80
        tableView.contentInset = UIEdgeInsets(top: 0, left: 0, bottom:
100, right: 0)
        view.addSubview(tableView)

        addButton.addTarget(self,
            action: "addTodoButtonPressed:",
            forControlEvents: .TouchUpInside)
        view.addSubview(addButton)
    }
}
```

The purpose of the `setup()` function is to configure and connect the UI components. In this case, the `tableview` component is inserted into the `views` hierarchy. Set the related cell, and set an inset value for the bottom, to allow the content of the view to scroll on top of the button, and connect to the data source and delegate. We also add a callback to the button:

```
// MARK: Layout
private extension TodosViewController{
    func layoutView(){
        layout(tableView) { view in
            view.top == view.superview!.top
            view.bottom == view.superview!.bottom
            view.left == view.superview!.left
            view.right == view.superview!.right
        }
        layout(addButton) { view in
            view.bottom == view.superview!.bottom - 5
            view.centerX == view.superview!.centerX
            view.width == view.height
            view.height == 60
        }
    }
}
```

The purpose of the `layoutView()` function is to define the `AutoLayout` constraints for each component.

AutoLayout is a really powerful way to handle the layout of a UI, but it can be very verbose and prone to trivial mistakes. To soften the burden of defining the constraints of AutoLayout, we use Cartography (`https://github.com/robb/Cartography`), a library that provides a clean and terse API to define the relationships between components and simplify the use of AutoLayout through code.

If we try to compile the app now, we get an error because Xcode doesn't find the definition of `layout()`. To solve this, we must import the `Cartography` framework.

```
import Cartography
```

We can move on to the last configuration function:

```
// MARK: Style
private extension TodosViewController{
    func style(){
        view.backgroundColor = UIColor.whiteColor()
        addButton.setImage(UIImage(named: "add-button"),
            forState: .Normal)
    }
}
```

The purpose of `style()` is to set all the colors, fonts, and images for the components.

It could seem like a useless increase of functions and call indirection, but when you get used to this structure; changing a constraint, modifying a label, or adding a component will be done in no time because you'll know exactly where to make a change.

To provide some data to be shown inside the table view, the datasource creates a stub cell:

```
// MARK: UITableViewDataSource
extension TodosViewController : UITableViewDataSource {
    func tableView(tableView: UITableView,
        numberOfRowsInSection section: Int) -> Int {
        return 10
    }
    func tableView(tableView: UITableView,
        cellForRowAtIndexPath indexPath: NSIndexPath) ->
UITableViewCell {
        let cell = tableView.dequeueReusableCellWithIdentifier("Cell")
            as! UITableViewCell
        cell.selectionStyle = .None
        cell.textLabel?.font = UIFont.latoLightFontOfSize(14)
        cell.textLabel?.text = "Todo number \(indexPath.row)"

        return cell
    }
}
```

Just to make the cell prettier, we changed the font to **Lato** (`https://www.google.com/fonts/specimen/Lato`), which is a nice open source font. Again, we need to import the `LatoFont` framework:

```
import LatoFont
```

Finally, we write an empty callback for the button:

```
// MARK: Actions
extension TodosViewController {
    func addTodoButtonPressed(sender: UIButton!){
        println("addTodoButtonPressed")
    }
}
```

When you run the app, it looks really nice, as shown in this screenshot:

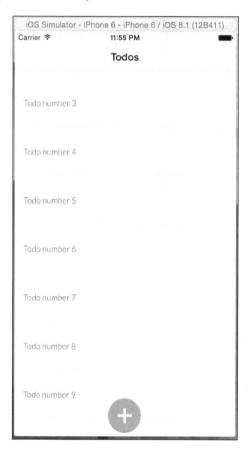

 You can find the code for this version at `https://github.com/gscalzo/Todolist/tree/skeleton_app`.

Building the Todos screen

Let's move on to populate the ViewController we have just created with the proper entities.

Adding the entities

The first thing we need to do is to create the entities, which is really straightforward. Basically, we just need to map the requested fields in a `struct`:

```swift
struct Todo: Equatable {
    let description: String
    let list: List
    let dueDate: NSDate
    let done: Bool
    let doneDate: NSDate?
}

func ==(todo1: Todo, todo2: Todo) -> Bool {
    return todo1.description == todo2.description
        && todo1.dueDate == todo2.dueDate
}
struct List {
    let description: String
}
```

Implementing the datastore

Next, we create the datastore to handle all the operations of the entities.

For now, we only return two lists of entities:

```swift
class TodosDatastore {
    private var savedLists = Array<List>()
    private var savedTodos = Array<Todo>()

    init(){
        savedLists = [
            List(description: "Personal"),
            List(description: "Work"),
            List(description: "Family")
        ]
        savedTodos = [
            Todo(description: "Remember the Milk",
                list: List(description: "Family") ,
                dueDate: NSDate(),
                done: false,
                doneDate: nil),
            Todo(description: "Buy Spider Man Comics",
                list: List(description: "Personal") ,
```

```
                    dueDate: NSDate(),
                    done: true,
                    doneDate: NSDate(),),
                Todo(description: "Release build",
                    list: List(description: "Work") ,
                    dueDate: NSDate(),
                    done: false,
                    doneDate: nil),
        ]
    }


    func todos() -> Array<Todo> {
        return savedTodos
    }

    func lists() -> Array<List> {
        return savedLists
    }
}
```

Connecting the datastore and the ViewController

Then we need to inject this datastore into the ViewController.

To do that, we create a couple of properties and we implement a init() function that accepts the datastore as a parameter:

```
private let todosDatastore: TodosDatastore
private var todos: Array<Todo>

private init() {
    fatalError("init() must not called")
}

required init(todosDatastore: TodosDatastore) {
    self.todosDatastore = todosDatastore
    self.todos = todosDatastore.todos()
    super.init(nibName: nil, bundle: nil)
}

internal required init(coder aDecoder: NSCoder) {
    fatalError("init(coder:) has not been implemented")
}
```

Note how, by using the `internal` and `private` keywords, we are forcing the client of this class to use the correct `init()`.

Because we have changed the signature of the `init()` function, we need to change the `UICellView` class that is instantiated in `AppDelegate`:

```
let viewController = TodosViewController(
                            todosDatastore: TodosDatastore())
```

The `Todo` tasks must be sorted by the date crescent, so we add a function to refresh the order of the `Todo` tasks:

```
override func viewWillAppear(animated: Bool) {
    super.viewWillAppear(animated)
    refresh()
}

private func refresh() {
    todos = todosDatastore.todos().sorted {
        $0.dueDate.compare($1.dueDate) ==
            NSComparisonResult.OrderedAscending}
    tableView.reloadData()
}
```

A closure may omit the name for its parameters. In this case, its parameters are implicitly named starting with $, followed by their position, such as: $0, $1, and so on.

Configuring tableView

First of all, we need to register the correct `CellView` class in `setup()`:

```
tableView.registerClass(TodoViewCell.classForCoder(),
                            forCellReuseIdentifier: "Cell")
```

Then, we change the datasource:

```
// MARK: UITableViewDataSource
extension TodosViewController : UITableViewDataSource {
    func tableView(tableView: UITableView,
        numberOfRowsInSection section: Int) -> Int {
        return todos.count
    }
    func tableView(tableView: UITableView,
                cellForRowAtIndexPath indexPath: NSIndexPath)
```

```
               -> UITableViewCell {
    let cell = tableView.dequeueReusableCellWithIdentifier("Cell")
      as! TodoViewCell
    let todo = todos[indexPath.row]
    cell.render(todo)
    cell.selectionStyle = .None

    return cell
  }
}
```

Basically, we are retrieving the correct `todo` task and passing it to a cell to render it.

Implementing TodoViewCell

At the top of the file, we import the required frameworks:

```
import UIKit
import Foundation
import Cartography
import FontAwesomeKit
```

As you can see, other than `Cartography`, we are importing `FontAwesomeKit` (`https://github.com/PrideChung/FontAwesomeKit`), which is a wrapper around `FontAwesome` (`http://fontawesome.io`), a nice collection of icons as a font.

We implement the same structure that we used in the ViewController to split the different responsibilities:

```
class TodoViewCell: UITableViewCell {
    private let subtitle = UILabel()
    private let title = UILabel()
    private let checkMark = UILabel()

    override func layoutSubviews() {
        super.layoutSubviews()
        setup()
        layoutView()
        style()
    }
}
```

This time, we have used the `layoutSubviews()` function as the starting point:

```
// MARK: Setup
private extension TodoViewCell{
    func setup(){
        contentView.addSubview(subtitle)
        title.numberOfLines = 0
        contentView.addSubview(title)
        contentView.addSubview(checkMark)
    }
}
```

Note that by setting the `numberOfLines` property to 0, we are setting the label as multiline, allowing us to have a length of more than one line for the `todo` task text.

The `setup()` functions just add the components to the parent view:

```
// MARK: Layout
private extension TodoViewCell{
    func layoutView(){
        layout(subtitle) { view in
            view.top    == view.superview!.top   + 10
            view.left   == view.superview!.left  + 10
            view.right == view.superview!.right - 10
            view.height == 20
        }

        layout(checkMark) { view in
            view.left == view.superview!.left + 10
            view.width == view.height
        }

        layout(title, subtitle) { view, view2 in
            view.top == view2.bottom
            return
        }

        layout(title, checkMark) { view, view2 in
            view.bottom == view.superview!.bottom - 5
            view.left == view2.right + 5
            view.right == view.superview!.right - 10
            view.centerY == view2.centerY
        }
    }
}
```

The `layoutView()` is a bit more verbose, but it doesn't do anything more than setting space relations between the components:

```
// MARK: Style
private extension TodoViewCell{
    func style(){
        contentView.backgroundColor = UIColor.clearColor()
        subtitle.textAlignment = .Left
        subtitle.font = UIFont.latoLightFontOfSize(14)
        title.textAlignment = .Left
        title.font = UIFont.latoFontOfSize(18)
        checkMark.textAlignment = .Center
    }
}
```

The `style()` function simply adds the fonts to the components.

Finally, the `render()` function extracts the values from the `todo` task and puts them into the labels:

```
// MARK: render
extension TodoViewCell{
    private func checkmarkAttributedStringTodo(todo: Todo) ->
NSAttributedString{
        var icon: FAKIcon!
        if todo.done {
            icon = FAKFontAwesome.checkSquareOIconWithSize(20)
        } else {
            icon = FAKFontAwesome.squareOIconWithSize(20)
        }
        return icon.attributedString()
    }

    func render(todo: Todo){
        let dateFormatter:NSDateFormatter = NSDateFormatter()
        dateFormatter.dateFormat = "HH:mm dd-MM-YY"
        let dueDate = dateFormatter.stringFromDate(todo.dueDate)

        subtitle.text = "\(dueDate) | \(todo.list.description)"
        title.text = todo.description

        checkMark.attributedText = checkmarkAttributedStringTodo(todo)
    }
}
```

Note how we are getting the checkbox icon from `FontAwesome` and putting the checkbox icon into the label as an attributed string.

Now, if we run the app, we can see how gorgeous it is, as shown in the following screenshot:

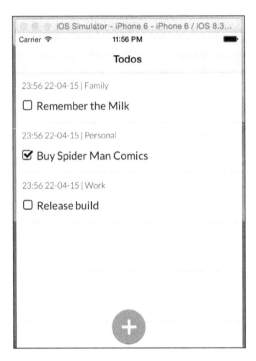

Note that CocoaPods makes integrating Objective-C and Swift libraries really straightforward. It basically creates frameworks, and the client app can simply import them, without worrying about which language was used to create them.

Swipe that cell!

The last thing missing in this screen is the swipeable cells.

Guess what? We are going to solve this problem using a pod — MGSwipeTableCell.

The `MGSwipeTableCell` (https://github.com/MortimerGoro/MGSwipeTableCell) pod is a really powerful and flexible add-on for `UITableViewCell`.

First of all, we add `MGSwipeTableCell` as the parent of our `TodoViewCell`:

```
import MGSwipeTableCell

class TodoViewCell: MGSwipeTableCell {
```

Then we configure the datasource by adding swipeable buttons to the cell:

```
cell.selectionStyle = .None
cell.rightButtons = [
    MGSwipeButton(title: "Edit",
        backgroundColor: UIColor.sunflower(),
            padding: 30) {
        [weak self] sender in
        self?.editButtonPressed(todo)
        return true
    },
    MGSwipeButton(title: "Delete",
        backgroundColor: UIColor.alizarin(),
            padding: 30) {
        [weak self] sender in
        self?.deleteButtonPressed(todo)
        return true
    }
]
cell.rightExpansion.buttonIndex = 0

cell.leftButtons = [
    MGSwipeButton(title: "Done",
        backgroundColor: UIColor.emerald(),
            padding: 30) {
        [weak self] sender in
        self?.doneButtonPressed(todo)
        return true
    }
]
cell.leftExpansion.buttonIndex = 0
return cell
```

One of the problems that can appear while using blocks in ARC is the creation of the strong retain cycle. If we remove the `[weak self]` from the implementation of the blocks, this is what will happen:

- The cell will own the button
- The button will own the block
- The block will own the cell

That means that none of these objects will be removed from memory when the cell is released by all of its clients.

By using [weak self], the cell is just assigned to the block instead of being passed with a strong reference (thus incrementing the reference counter for the cell), without incrementing the reference counter. In this way, the cycle is not completed.

As the weak reference creates an optional variable, to use self, we must use the question mark, which doesn't call the method if the variable is nil. Just to make the app prettier, we reuse the flat UI color we used in the previous app:

```
import UIKit
extension UIColor {
    class func separatorColor() -> UIColor {
        return UIColor.colorComponents((209, 209, 212))
    }
    class func greenSea() -> UIColor {
        return UIColor.colorComponents((22, 160, 133))
    }
    class func emerald() -> UIColor {
        return UIColor.colorComponents((46, 204, 113))
    }
    class func sunflower() -> UIColor {
        return UIColor.colorComponents((241, 196, 15))
    }
    class func alizarin() -> UIColor {
        return UIColor.colorComponents((231, 76, 60))
    }
}
private extension UIColor {
    class func colorComponents(components: (CGFloat, CGFloat,
CGFloat)) -> UIColor {
        return UIColor(red: components.0/255, green: components.1/255,
blue: components.2/255, alpha: 1)
    }
}
```

After creating the button, we need to extend the actions for the ViewController to handle the buttons:

```
// MARK: Actions
extension TodosViewController {
    func addTodoButtonPressed(sender: UIButton!){
        println("addTodoButtonPressed")
    }

    func editButtonPressed(todo: Todo){
        println("editButtonPressed")
    }

    func deleteButtonPressed(todo: Todo){
        todosDatastore.deleteTodo(todo)
        refresh()
    }

    func doneButtonPressed(todo: Todo){
        todosDatastore.doneTodo(todo)
        refresh()
    }
}
```

Finally, we create the empty methods inside the datastore:

```
// MARK: Actions
extension TodosDatastore {
    func addTodo(todo: Todo) {
        println("addTodo")
    }

    func deleteTodo(todo: Todo?) {
        println("deleteTodo")
    }

    func doneTodo(todo: Todo) {
        println("doneTodo")
    }
}
```

By running the app, we can see that we have implemented all of the requested features for the first screen:

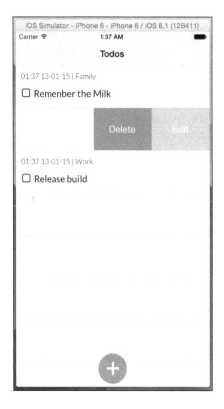

 You can find the code at `https://github.com/gscalzo/ Todolist/tree/todos_screen`.

Adding a Todo task

So far, the app works very well, presenting all the `Todo` tasks, but we need to allow the user to create their own `Todo` task.

The add a Todo ViewController

As the specifications require that a `Todo` task be editable, it does make sense to use the same ViewController, either to create a new `Todo` task, or to edit an already existing `Todo` task. First of all, we need to implement the `addTodoButtonPressed()` action:

```
func addTodoButtonPressed(sender: UIButton!){
  let addTodoVC = EditTodoViewController(todosDatastore:
todosDatastore, todoToEdit: nil)
  addTodoVC.title = "New Todo"
  navigationController!.pushViewController(addTodoVC, animated: true)
}
```

Let's implement `editButtonPressed()` as well:

```
func editButtonPressed(todo: Todo){
let editTodoVC = EditTodoViewController(todosDatastore:
todosDatastore, todoToEdit: todo)
editTodoVC.title = "Edit Todo"
navigationController!.pushViewController(editTodoVC, animated: true)
}
```

As you can see, the differences between the actions are only in the title of the ViewController and in the `Todo` task passed as a parameter. In the case of the `addTodoButtonPressed()`, the `todoTask` object passed is `nitl`, this means that a new `Todo` task will be created.

The `EditTodoViewController` has a few components for rendering it, as expected:

```
class EditTodoViewController: UIViewController {
    private let descriptionTextField = UITextField()
    private let descriptionSeparator = UIView()
    private let listNameLabel = UILabel()
    private let listButton = UIButton()
    private let listSeparator = UIView()
    private let dueDateLabel = UILabel()
    private let dueDateButton = UIButton()
    private let dueDateSeparator = UIView()
    private let doneButton = UIButton()
  private let dueDatePicker = UIDatePicker()
```

We also need to set a few properties required for constructing or editing a `Todo` task:

```
    private let todosDatastore: TodosDatastore
    private let todoToEdit: Todo?
    private var list: List
    private var dueDate: NSDate
```

Then, we define the required initializers — empty initializers:

```
private init() {
    fatalError("init() must not called")
}
required init(coder aDecoder: NSCoder) {
    fatalError("init(coder:) has not been implemented")
}
```

The required constructor accepts the datastore and an optional `Todo` task:

```
required init(todosDatastore: TodosDatastore, todoToEdit: Todo?) {
    self.todosDatastore = todosDatastore
    self.todoToEdit = todoToEdit
    if let todo = self.todoToEdit {
        descriptionTextField.text = todo.description
        list = todo.list
        dueDate = todo.dueDate
    } else {
        list = self.todosDatastore.defaultList()
        dueDate = self.todosDatastore.defaultDueDate()
    }
    super.init(nibName: nil, bundle: nil)
}
```

This becomes the designed initializer. Therefore, to instantiate an object of this type, you must call this initializer. Required initializers are generally used when you plan to extend a class, and all the subclasses must implement the required initializer.

When the optional `Todo` contains an actual value, the fields from that value are extracted to initialize the fields. Otherwise, the default values are provided.

As you can see, the default values aren't set directly in the ViewController code. Instead, the ViewController asks for the default values of `lists` and `duedate` from the datastore, giving it the responsibility to handle them.

This distinction, which can seem confusing, is really important. The default values are from the domain of the data not from the domain of the presentation, and the proper place is in the datastore.

Let's implement them in `TodosDatastore`:

```
func defaultList() -> List {
    return List(description: "Personal")
}
```

```
func defaultDueDate() -> NSDate {
    let now = NSDate()
    let secondsInADay = NSTimeInterval(24 * 60 * 60)
    return now.dateByAddingTimeInterval(secondsInADay)
}
```

Because the default list is always present, we change the `lists()` function accordingly:

```
func lists() -> Array<List> {
    return [defaultList()] + savedLists
}
```

But now, let's go back to `EditTodoViewController`, implementing `viewDidLoad()` using the structure we have already seen:

```
override func viewDidLoad() {
    super.viewDidLoad()

    setup()
    layoutView()
    style()
}
```

As we have a lot of components, `setup()` and `layoutView()` can easily become a mess, so we'll exploit a nice feature of Swift—functions inside functions:

```
// MARK: Setup
private extension EditTodoViewController{
    func setup(){
        func descriptionSetup() {}
        func listSetup() {
        func dueDateSetup() {}
        func doneSetup() {}
        func datePickerSetup() {

        descriptionSetup()
        listSetup()
        dueDateSetup()
        doneSetup()
        datePickerSetup()
        refresh()
    }
}
```

This trick allows us to have all the related pieces of code tied together.

Implementing each function is straightforward:

```
func descriptionSetup() {
  descriptionTextField.placeholder = "Description of Todo"
  descriptionTextField.becomeFirstResponder()
  view.addSubview(descriptionTextField)
         view.addSubview(descriptionSeparator)
}
```

Regarding the `textField` description, the only thing to notice is the call of `becomeFirstResponder()`, which gives the focus to the fields and forces the keyboard to appear:

```
func listSetup() {
        view.addSubview(listNameLabel)
        listButton.setAttributedTitle(FAKFontAwesome.
listIconWithSize(20).attributedString(), forState: .Normal)
        listButton.addTarget(self, action: "listButtonPressed:",
forControlEvents: .TouchUpInside)
        view.addSubview(listButton)
        view.addSubview(listSeparator)
}

func dueDateSetup() {
        view.addSubview(dueDateLabel)
        dueDateButton.setAttributedTitle(FAKFontAwesome.
clockOIconWithSize(20).attributedString(), forState: .Normal)
        dueDateButton.addTarget(self, action:
"dueDateButtonPressed:", forControlEvents: .TouchUpInside)
        view.addSubview(dueDateButton)
        view.addSubview(dueDateSeparator)
}

func doneSetup() {
        doneButton.setAttributedTitle(FAKFontAwesome.
checkIconWithSize(80).attributedString(), forState: .Normal)
        doneButton.addTarget(self, action: "doneButtonPressed:",
forControlEvents: .TouchUpInside)
        view.addSubview(doneButton)
}
```

The setup of the other components is pretty simple; we just have to add them to the view and connect a callback for when the button is pressed:

```
func datePickerSetup() {
        dueDatePicker.datePickerMode = .DateAndTime
```

```
            dueDatePicker.minimumDate = NSDate()
            dueDatePicker.date = dueDate
            dueDatePicker.addTarget(self, action: "dueDateChanged:",
    forControlEvents: .ValueChanged)
            view.addSubview(dueDatePicker)
        }
```

The picker needs a similar piece of code, just setting the kind of picker and the minimum and actual dates, and connecting a function when the value changes:

```
    func refresh() {
        listNameLabel.text = "List: \(list.description)"

        let dateFormatter:NSDateFormatter = NSDateFormatter()
        dateFormatter.dateFormat = "HH:mm dd-MM-YY"
        let formattedDueDate = dateFormatter.stringFromDate(dueDate)
        dueDateLabel.text = "Due date: \(formattedDueDate)"
    }
```

The `refresh()` function sets the value of the components, given the models, and it will be called when a model changes.

Moving on to the layout, we see that the code is pretty boring: it's just a matter of defining the constraints without missing any, or adding conflicts among them:

```
// MARK: Layout
private extension EditTodoViewController{
    func layoutView(){
        func descriptionLayout() {
            layout(descriptionTextField) { view in
                view.top == view.superview!.top + 70
                view.left == view.superview!.left + 10
                view.right == view.superview!.right - 10
                view.height == 50
            }

            layout(descriptionSeparator, descriptionTextField) {view,
    view2 in
                view.left == view.superview!.left
                view.right == view.superview!.right
                view.top == view2.bottom
                view.height == 1
            }
        }

        func listLayout() {
```

```
                layout(listNameLabel, descriptionSeparator) {view, view2
    in
            view.top == view2.bottom
            return
        }


                layout(listNameLabel, descriptionTextField) {view, view2
    in
            view.left == view2.left
            view.height == view2.height
        }


                layout(listNameLabel, listButton) {view, view2 in
            view.right == view2.left
            view.top == view2.top
            view.height == view2.height
            view2.height == view2.width
            view2.right == view2.superview!.right
        }


                layout(listSeparator, listNameLabel) {view, view2 in
            view.left == view.superview!.left
            view.right == view.superview!.right
            view.top == view2.bottom
            view.height == 1
        }
    }

    func dueDateLayout() {
        layout(dueDateLabel, listSeparator) {view, view2 in
            view.top == view2.bottom
            return
        }


        layout(dueDateLabel, listNameLabel) {view, view2 in
            view.left == view2.left
            view.height == view2.height
        }


        layout(dueDateLabel, dueDateButton) {view, view2 in
            view.right == view2.left
            view.top == view2.top
            view.height == view2.height
            view2.height == view2.width
```

```
                    view2.right == view2.superview!.right
                }

                layout(dueDateSeparator, dueDateLabel) {view, view2 in
                    view.left == view.superview!.left
                    view.right == view.superview!.right
                    view.top == view2.bottom
                    view.height == 1
                }
            }

        func doneLayout() {
            layout(doneButton, dueDateSeparator) {view, view2 in
                view.top == view2.bottom + 20
                view.centerX == view.superview!.centerX
                view.height == view.width
                view.width == 100
            }
        }

        func datePickerLayout() {
            layout(dueDatePicker) {view in
                view.left == view.superview!.left
                view.right == view.superview!.right
                view.bottom == view.superview!.bottom
            }
        }

        descriptionLayout()
        listLayout()
        dueDateLayout()
        doneLayout()
        datePickerLayout()


    }
}
```

The usual trick allows us to modularize the code, which otherwise, could have been a mess.

The `style()` sets the colors and the font of the components:

```
// MARK: Style
private extension EditTodoViewController{
    func style(){
```

```
            view.backgroundColor = UIColor.whiteColor()
            descriptionTextField.font = UIFont.latoLightFontOfSize(20)
            descriptionTextField.backgroundColor = UIColor.whiteColor()
            descriptionSeparator.backgroundColor = UIColor.
    separatorColor()

            listNameLabel.font = UIFont.latoFontOfSize(16)
            listNameLabel.backgroundColor = UIColor.whiteColor()
            listSeparator.backgroundColor = UIColor.separatorColor()

            dueDateLabel.font = UIFont.latoFontOfSize(16)
            dueDateLabel.backgroundColor = UIColor.whiteColor()
            dueDateSeparator.backgroundColor = UIColor.separatorColor()
        }
    }
```

We have just defined a new color using the same default value in the separator of the cells of a TableView:

```
        class func separatorColor() -> UIColor {
            return UIColor.colorComponents((209, 209, 212))
        }
```

Finally, we can implement the actions, starting from `listButtonPressed()`, where we create a new ViewController and put it on top of the stack:

```
        func listButtonPressed(sender: UIButton!){
            let listsVC = ListsViewController(todosDatastore:
    todosDatastore) { list in
                self.list = list
                self.refresh()
            }
            navigationController!.pushViewController(listsVC, animated:
    true)
        }
```

As you can see, we are passing a block as the last argument—a block that will be called when the user has selected the list. The remaining actions are really straightforward and don't need any further explanation:

```
    func dueDateButtonPressed(sender: UIButton!) {
            descriptionTextField.resignFirstResponder()
        }

        func doneButtonPressed(sender: UIButton!) {
            if !descriptionTextField.text.isEmpty {
```

```
        let newTodo = Todo(description: descriptionTextField.text,
            list: list,
            dueDate: dueDate,
            done: false,
            doneDate: nil)
        todosDatastore.addTodo(newTodo)
        todosDatastore.deleteTodo(todoToEdit)
        navigationController!.popViewControllerAnimated(true)
    }
}

func dueDateChanged(sender: UIButton!) {
    dueDate = dueDatePicker.date
    refresh()
}
```

Updating the datastore

Before finishing, we need to implement the actions in the datastore to update Todo,
paying attention to the use of immutable entities:

```
func addTodo(todo: Todo) {
    savedTodos = savedTodos + [todo]
}

func deleteTodo(todo: Todo?) {
    if let todo = todo {
        savedTodos = savedTodos.filter({$0 != todo})
    }
}

func doneTodo(todo: Todo) {
    deleteTodo(todo)
    let doneTodo = Todo(description: todo.description,
        list: todo.list,
        dueDate:
        todo.dueDate,
        done: true,
        doneDate: NSDate())
    addTodo(doneTodo)
}
```

With this code, we have completed the `EditTodoViewController`, and the user can finally create a `Todo` task.

Adding a list

One more feature missing is the ability to create and set a list.

Implementing ListViewCell

As you can imagine, much of the code is just boilerplate, so we won't spend much time on it. Let's start with `ListViewCell`:

```
class ListViewCell: UITableViewCell {
    private let title = UILabel()

    override func layoutSubviews() {
        super.layoutSubviews()
        setup()
        layoutView()
        style()
    }
}
```

```
// MARK: Setup
private extension ListViewCell{
    func setup(){
        title.numberOfLines = 0
        contentView.addSubview(title)
    }
}

// MARK: Layout
private extension ListViewCell{
    func layoutView(){
        layout(title) { view in
            view.top == view.superview!.top + 5
            view.bottom == view.superview!.bottom - 5
            view.left == view.superview!.left + 15
            view.right == view.superview!.right - 10
        }
    }
}

// MARK: Style
private extension ListViewCell{
    func style(){
        contentView.backgroundColor = UIColor.clearColor()
        title.textAlignment = .Left
        title.font = UIFont.latoLightFontOfSize(18)
    }
}

// MARK: render
extension ListViewCell{
    func render(list: List){
        title.text = list.description
    }
}
```

Everything is pretty clear once you are used to this kind of class structure.

Building ListViewController

We perform steps similar to the preceding heading for `ListViewController`:

```swift
class ListsViewController: UIViewController {
    private let tableView = UITableView()
    private let addButton = UIButton()

    private let todosDatastore: TodosDatastore
    private let onListSelected: (list: List) -> Void

    private init() {
        fatalError("init() must not called")
    }

    required init(todosDatastore: TodosDatastore, onListSelected:
(list: List) -> Void) {
        self.todosDatastore = todosDatastore
        self.onListSelected = onListSelected
        super.init(nibName: nil, bundle: nil)
    }

    required init(coder aDecoder: NSCoder) {
        fatalError("init(coder:) has not been implemented")
    }

    override func viewDidLoad() {
        super.viewDidLoad()

        setup()
        layoutView()
        style()
    }
}
```

After creating the skeleton of the class, let's proceed with creating the usual extensions:

```swift
// MARK: Setup
private extension ListsViewController{
    func setup(){
        title = "Lists"
        tableView.registerClass(ListViewCell.classForCoder(),
forCellReuseIdentifier: "Cell")
        tableView.dataSource = self
        tableView.delegate = self
        tableView.rowHeight = 50
```

```
        tableView.contentInset = UIEdgeInsets(top: 10, left: 0,
bottom: 100, right: 0)
        view.addSubview(tableView)

        addButton.addTarget(self, action: "addListButtonPressed:",
forControlEvents: .TouchUpInside)
        view.addSubview(addButton)
    }
}
```

The setup extension builds the table view and sets it on the main view of the
ViewController:

```
// MARK: Layout
private extension ListsViewController{
    func layoutView(){
        layout(tableView) { view in
            view.top == view.superview!.top
            view.bottom == view.superview!.bottom
            view.left == view.superview!.left
            view.right == view.superview!.right
        }
        layout(addButton) { view in
            view.bottom == view.superview!.bottom - 5
            view.centerX == view.superview!.centerX
            view.width == view.height
            view.height == 60
        }
    }
}


// MARK: Style
private extension ListsViewController{
    func style(){
        view.backgroundColor = UIColor.whiteColor()
        addButton.setImage(UIImage(named: "add-button"), forState:
.Normal)
    }
}
```

The layout and style extensions set up the table view and the button in the same way as we did for the `TodoViewController`:

```swift
// MARK: UITableViewDataSource
extension ListsViewController : UITableViewDataSource {
    func tableView(tableView: UITableView, numberOfRowsInSection
section: Int) -> Int {
        return todosDatastore.lists().count
    }
    func tableView(tableView: UITableView, cellForRowAtIndexPath
indexPath: NSIndexPath) -> UITableViewCell {
        let cell = tableView.dequeueReusableCellWithIdentifier("Cell")
as! ListViewCell
        let list = todosDatastore.lists()[indexPath.row]
        cell.render(list)
        cell.selectionStyle = .None
        return cell
    }
}
```

The datasource creates a cell that retrieves the value of the list from the datastore:

```swift
// MARK: UITableViewDelegate
extension ListsViewController : UITableViewDelegate {
    func tableView(tableView: UITableView, didSelectRowAtIndexPath
indexPath: NSIndexPath) {
        let list = todosDatastore.lists()[indexPath.row]
        onListSelected(list: list)
        navigationController?.popViewControllerAnimated(true)
    }
}
```

The delegate calls the closure we passed during the creation, to set the list into the view creating the `Todo`. Finally, `addListButtonPressed()` asks the user the name of the list to create:

```swift
// MARK: Actions
extension ListsViewController {
    func addListButtonPressed(sender: UIButton!){
        var alert = UIAlertController(title: "Enter list name",
            message: "To create a new list, please enter the name of
the list",
            preferredStyle: .Alert)

        let okAction = UIAlertAction(title: "OK",
            style: .Default) { (action: UIAlertAction!) -> Void in
```

```
                    let textField = alert.textFields![0] as! UITextField
                    self.addList(textField.text)
            }

        let cancelAction = UIAlertAction(title: "Cancel",
            style: .Default, handler: nil)

        alert.addAction(okAction)
        alert.addAction(cancelAction)

        alert.addTextFieldWithConfigurationHandler(nil)

        presentViewController(alert,
            animated: true,
            completion: nil)

    }

    private func addList(description: NSString) {
        todosDatastore.addListDescription(description as String)
        tableView.reloadData()
    }
}
```

To let the user insert a new list name, we use a simple `AlertView` with two buttons—**Ok** and **Cancel**—and a text field.

With the new UIAlertController introduced in iOS 8, it is just a matter of defining two `UIAlertAction` components, where the **Cancel** button has an empty handler because it must only dismiss the alert view, and a text field without any handler because the inserted value has already been retrieved by the handler of the **Ok** button.

Updating the datastore

Obviously, we need to implement the missing `addListDescription()` function in the datastore of the `Todo` tasks:

```
func addListDescription(description: String) {
    if !description.isEmpty {
        savedLists = savedLists + [List(description: description)]
    }
}
```

We need also to remove the `init()` method, which creates fake records.

 You can find the code at `https://github.com/gscalzo/Todolist/tree/feature_complete`.

Where do we go from here?

The app looks nice, but there is a lot to improve, starting with the persistence layer.

There are several ways to save data in an iOS app. None of them are straightforward, so they are beyond the scope of this book. Yet, you can find two different ways to make data persist in the master branch (one method uses a file to persist the data, the other uses `CoreData`, a library to manage data in a database).

 You can find the complete source code of the app at `https://github.com/gscalzo/Todolist/tree/feature_complete`.

Another cool thing to implement is to add local notifications when the `Todo` task reaches the due date. Adding is also a quick way to increase the due date; you can add 10 minutes, 1 hour, or 1 day.

Summary

You must have thought that developing with Swift makes creating an app straightforward, right? Unfortunately, it does not. This long chapter showed that most of the coding is devoted to configuring components of the SDK and creating connections between the classes of our app, instead of using cool functional programming tricks.

However, in this chapter, we covered most of the aspects that an iOS developer must know, starting with CocoaPods, to laying out the components of the views and differentiating responsibilities between the different layers of an app.

Another important skill you need to learn is how to connect to a server to retrieve data—a server that could be either under our control, or a third-party server, such as a service.

In the next chapter, you'll learn how to exploit external servers to add content to an app, and retrieving and sending JSON data. We'll pack this technique to create a pretty weather app.

$$4$$

A Pretty Weather App

In the previous chapter, when we developed the To-do list, we mentioned that a connection with a remote server was the tool that was missing from the common iOS developer tool set we were covering.

In this chapter, we are going to fill this gap, showing you how to retrieve data from two different remote services.

We'll also implement an app that solves a real problem using most of the techniques that we have already seen in the previous chapter.

The app is…

One of the key facts of the mobile revolution is that we always have in our pocket a computer that constantly uses GPS, to which we can ask anything regarding everything around us.

As we can see by searching the App Store, forecasting weather is a common problem that apps try to solve, often using stunning designs, but sometimes using a basic design with a lot a features. This confuses the user.

If we look carefully at the nicest, and most famous, weather apps, we realize that the structures are really similar, and this is the kind of app we want to build.

Although a few apps allow you to check the weather of several cities at a time, for simplicity, we'll implement an app that shows only the weather of your current city.

That said, the aim of the app is—first of all—to show the current weather for the current location, and then to show the forecast for the upcoming hours and days.

To make the app more appealing, we'll add a nice photo of the current city as the background. The following screenshot shows the wireframe of the first page:

Basically, the information needed for this view includes the temperature (current, maximum, and minimum) and a description of the current weather.

When we slide the scroll view up, the forecasts appear. At the top, in a horizontal scroll view, there is an hourly forecast for the current day. Below it is a list of the forecast for the days of the following week, showing the temperature and weather icons, as shown here:

Because the scroll view is transparent, to increase the contrast with the underneath image, we add a blur effect to the image itself.

Building the skeleton

Having defined the requirements, let's start implementing it, splitting the implementation into auto-conclusive phases.

Creating the project

In the same way as we did for the previous apps, we create an empty Single View app, from which we remove the reference to the main storyboard and the **ViewController** template.

Just for the sake of testing quickly, we create `PrettyWeatherViewController`, showing a red background:

```
class PrettyWeatherViewController: UIViewController {
    override func viewDidLoad() {
        super.viewDidLoad()
        view.backgroundColor = UIColor.redColor()
    }
}
```

Also, we add the creation of the ViewController in the AppDelegate:

```
func application(application: UIApplication,
didFinishLaunchingWithOptions launchOptions: [NSObject: AnyObject]?)
-> Bool {
    let viewController = PrettyWeatherViewController()

    let mainWindow = UIWindow(frame: UIScreen.mainScreen().bounds)
    mainWindow.backgroundColor = UIColor.whiteColor()
    mainWindow.rootViewController = viewController
    mainWindow.makeKeyAndVisible()
    window = mainWindow

    return true
}
```

If we run the app, a red background is the only thing we see. Let's now install CocoaPods, creating a Podfile with these pods:

```
use_frameworks!

target 'PrettyWeather' do
  pod 'Cartography', '~> 0.5'
  pod 'Alamofire', '~> 1.2'
  pod 'SwiftyJSON', '~> 2.2.0'
  pod 'WeatherIconsKit', :git => 'git@github.com:gscalzo/
WeatherIconsKit.git'
  pod 'FlickrKit', '~> 1.0.4'
  pod 'FXBlurView', '~> 1.6.3'
  pod 'LatoFont', :git => "https://github.com/gscalzo/LatoFont.git"
end
```

After running the pod installation, we have all the required libraries.

Adding the assets

Before moving to implement the scaffold of the UI, we add the icon and the default background image that is presented while we are downloading the one relative to the current location.

 The assets can be downloaded from `https://github.com/ gscalzo/PrettyWeather/blob/master/assets/assets. zip?raw=true`.

Put the icon and the default image into the Asset Catalogue, and the move to implement `PrettyWeatherViewController`:

```
import UIKit
import Cartography

class PrettyWeatherViewController: UIViewController {
    private let backgroundView = UIImageView()

    override func viewDidLoad() {
        super.viewDidLoad()
        setup()
        layoutView()
        style()
        render(UIImage(named: "DefaultImage"))
    }
}
```

The top part of the controller just builds all the structure components when the ViewController has loaded:

```
// MARK: Setup
private extension PrettyWeatherViewController{
    func setup(){
        backgroundView.contentMode = .ScaleAspectFill
        backgroundView.clipsToBounds = true
        view.addSubview(backgroundView)
    }
}
```

The only graphic component of the ViewController is the background image view, which is configured to contain the image to fulfill it completely:

```
// MARK: Layout
extension PrettyWeatherViewController{
    func layoutView() {
        layout(backgroundView) { view in
            view.top == view.superview!.top
            view.bottom == view.superview!.bottom
            view.left == view.superview!.left
            view.right == view.superview!.right
        }
    }
}
```

Being the background, the image view must occupy the entire screen. For the time being, the render just puts the image inside the image view:

```
// MARK: Render
private extension PrettyWeatherViewController{
    func render(image: UIImage?){
        if let image = image {
            backgroundView.image = image
        }
    }
}
```

Finally, an empty `style` function is added for uniformity with our structure:

```
// MARK: Style
private extension PrettyWeatherViewController{
    func style(){
    }
}
```

To complete the skeleton app, let's remove the status bar.

To do this, we need to open the configuration `.plist` file, called `Info.plist,` and add two keys: set `Status bar is initially hidden` to `YES`, and set `View controller-based status bar appearance` to `NO`.

Now, on running the app, the interface is what we expected, as shown in the following screenshot:

 You can find the code for this version at `https://github.com/gscalzo/PrettyWeather/tree/app_skeleton`.

Implementing the UI

A UI that is not as complicated as the one required can be really difficult to implement if we don't take the correct precautions.

A good way to minimize the complexity is to split the problem into more manageable subproblems, so we'll define three subviews: currentWeather, hourlyForecast, and dailyForecast. We'll implement them as separate entities. The following screenshot shows the view's structure:

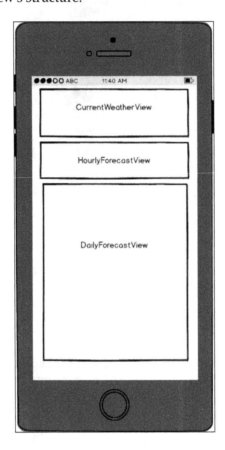

The UI in blocks

As just said, we implement the UI by creating three custom views, whose size and position we are temporarily hardcoding.

Let's start with CurrentWeatherView, adding it to PrettyWeatherViewController:

```
private let scrollView = UIScrollView()
private let currentWeatherView = CurrentWeatherView(frame:
CGRectZero)
```

As the height of the three elements is more than the height of the view, we create a scroll view to contain them:

```
func setup(){
    //...
    scrollView.showsVerticalScrollIndicator = false
    scrollView.addSubview(currentWeatherView)
    view.addSubview(scrollView)
}
```

The `setup()` function just adds the components to the views hierarchy:

```
func layoutView() {
    //...
    layout(scrollView) { view in
        view.top == view.superview!.top
        view.bottom == view.superview!.bottom
        view.left == view.superview!.left
        view.right == view.superview!.right
    }
    layout(currentWeatherView) { view in
        view.width == view.superview!.width
        view.centerX == view.superview!.centerX
    }
}
```

The layout basically centers the subview in the scroll view. Let's move on to `CustomView`:

```
class CurrentWeatherView: UIView {
    private var didSetupConstraints = false
    override init(frame: CGRect) {
        super.init(frame: frame)
        setup()
        style()
    }

    required init(coder aDecoder: NSCoder) {
        fatalError("init(coder:) has not been implemented")
    }

    override func updateConstraints() {
        if didSetupConstraints {
            super.updateConstraints()
            return
        }
        layoutView()
```

```
        super.updateConstraints()
        didSetupConstraints = true
    }
}
```

Here, the only difference from the usual structure is that `layoutView()` is not called during the initialization, but in the overridden method, `updateConstraints()`. This method is called by the framework when all other constraints are set and the view needs to be laid out. If you try to move the `layoutView()` call into the `init` method, you will see that the constraints will conflict.

Also, because `updateConstraints()` can be called more than once, we need to ensure that the constraints are not added multiple times:

```
// MARK: Setup
private extension CurrentWeatherView{
    func setup(){
    }
}

// MARK: Layout
private extension CurrentWeatherView{
    func layoutView(){
        layout(self) { view in
            view.height == 160
            return
        }
    }
}

// MARK: Style
private extension CurrentWeatherView{
    func style(){
        backgroundColor = UIColor.redColor()
    }
}
```

The `setup()` function is just an empty method; `layout()` defines the height, and `style()` paints the view red. If you run the app now, you will see a red rectangle at the top of the view. However, we wanted the view at the bottom. Also, the scroll view is not scrollable.

Before fixing this issue, here's a quick note on how scrollView works: the frame of a scrollView is the frame of the viewport that makes the content visible. Inside a scrollView, there is another view that contains the actual subviews. If the contentView is smaller than the scrollView, this one is not scrollable.

So, if we want to change the position of currentWeatherView, we need to lay it out inside the contentView. To do this, we add the following code to layoutView() of PrettyWeatherViewController:

```
let currentWeatherInsect: Float =
   Float(view.frame.height) -
   Float(currentWeatherView.frame.height) - 10
layout(currentWeatherView) { view in
 view.top == view.superview!.top + currentWeatherInsect
 return
}
```

When we run the app now, we can see that the view is in the correct position.

Implementing the two missing views is straightforward. First of all, we add the instances:

```
    private let hourlyForecastView = WeatherHourlyForecastView(frame:
CGRectZero)
    private let daysForecastView = WeatherDaysForecastView(frame:
CGRectZero)
```

Then, we add the views to the scrollView:

```
      scrollView.addSubview(hourlyForecastView)
      scrollView.addSubview(daysForecastView)
```

Finally, we lay them out:

```
      layout(hourlyForecastView, currentWeatherView) { view, view2
  in
        view.top == view2.bottom + 20
        view.width == view.superview!.width
        view.centerX == view.superview!.centerX
      }

      layout(daysForecastView, hourlyForecastView) { view, view2 in
        view.top == view2.bottom
        view.width == view2.width
        view.bottom == view.superview!.bottom - 20
        view.centerX == view.superview!.centerX
      }
```

The three views are stacked on top of each other. The only thing to note is that the bottom of `daysForecastView` is connected to the bottom of the scrollView, with the effect that enlarges the ContentView and makes the view scrollable.

 You can find the code for this version at `https://github.com/gscalzo/PrettyWeather/tree/ui_in_blocks`.

Completing the UI

Although the views are in the correct place, we need to implement all the components.

CurrentWeatherView

First of all, we need to import the fonts' frameworks:

```
import LatoFont
import WeatherIconsKit
```

The former is the font we've already used in the TodoList app; the latter is similar to AwesomeKit, and it contains a series of icons related to the weather:

```
private let cityLbl = UILabel()
private let maxTempLbl = UILabel()
private let minTempLbl = UILabel()
private let iconLbl = UILabel()
private let weatherLbl = UILabel()
private let currentTempLbl = UILabel()
```

We simply add all the labels and lay them out:

```
func layoutView(){
    layout(self) { view in
        view.height == 160
    }
    layout(iconLbl) { view in
        view.top == view.superview!.top
        view.left == view.superview!.left + 20
        view.width == 30
        view.width == view.height
    }
    layout(weatherLbl, iconLbl) { view, view2 in
        view.top == view2.top
        view.left == view2.right + 10
        view.height == view2.height
        view.width == 200
    }

    layout(currentTempLbl, iconLbl) { view, view2 in
        view.top == view2.bottom
        view.left == view2.left
    }

    layout(currentTempLbl, minTempLbl) { view, view2 in
        view.bottom == view2.top
        view.left == view2.left
    }
```

```
layout(minTempLbl) { view in
    view.bottom == view.superview!.bottom
    view.height == 30
}

layout(maxTempLbl, minTempLbl) { view, view2 in
    view.top == view2.top
    view.height == view2.height
    view.left == view2.right + 10
}
layout(cityLbl) { view in
    view.bottom == view.superview!.bottom
    view.right == view.superview!.right - 10
    view.height == 30
    view.width == 200
}
}
```

As usual, the layout part is the longest, and is full of boilerplate code:

```
func style(){
    iconLbl.textColor = UIColor.whiteColor()
    weatherLbl.font = UIFont.latoLightFontOfSize(20)
    weatherLbl.textColor = UIColor.whiteColor()

    currentTempLbl.font = UIFont.latoLightFontOfSize(96)
    currentTempLbl.textColor = UIColor.whiteColor()

    maxTempLbl.font = UIFont.latoLightFontOfSize(18)
    maxTempLbl.textColor = UIColor.whiteColor()

    minTempLbl.font = UIFont.latoLightFontOfSize(18)
    minTempLbl.textColor = UIColor.whiteColor()

    cityLbl.font = UIFont.latoLightFontOfSize(18)
    cityLbl.textColor = UIColor.whiteColor()
    cityLbl.textAlignment = .Right
}
```

In the `style()` function, we set the correct font and color, and finally set a `render()` function with dummy values:

```
// MARK: Render
extension CurrentWeatherView{
    func render(){
```

```
        iconLbl.attributedText = WIKFontIcon.
wiDaySunnyIconWithSize(20).attributedString()
        weatherLbl.text = "Sunny"

        minTempLbl.text = "4°"
        maxTempLbl.text = "10°"
        currentTempLbl.text = "6°"

        cityLbl.text = "London"
    }
}
```

Don't forget to call the render in `PrettyWeatherViewController`:

```
// MARK: Render
private extension PrettyWeatherViewController{
    func renderSubviews() {
        currentWeatherView.render()
    }
}
```

When we run the app, we can see that the view is shown in the correct place, with the correct info and style. But, because of the color, the label is not contrasting enough with the background, and it's difficult to read the data.

To solve this problem, we add a semi-transparent view between the background and the scrollView with a dark gradient that fades to completely transparent at the top.

To do this, we create an instance of UIView:

```
    private let gradientView = UIView()
```

Next, we add it to the view in `setup()`:

```
    view.addSubview(gradientView)
```

Then, we set the constraints:

```
        layout(gradientView) { view in
            view.top == view.superview!.top
            view.bottom == view.superview!.bottom
            view.left == view.superview!.left
            view.right == view.superview!.right
        }
```

In the `style` function, we set the gradient:

```
func style(){
    gradientView.backgroundColor = UIColor(white: 0, alpha: 0.7)
    let gradientLayer = CAGradientLayer()
    gradientLayer.frame = gradientView.bounds

    let blackColor = UIColor(white: 0, alpha: 0.0)
    let clearColor = UIColor(white: 0, alpha: 1.0)

    gradientLayer.colors = [blackColor.CGColor, clearColor.
CGColor]

    gradientLayer.startPoint = CGPointMake(1.0, 0.5)
    gradientLayer.endPoint = CGPointMake(1.0, 1.0)
    gradientView.layer.mask = gradientLayer
}
```

If we run the app now, we can see that the data is more readable.

WeatherHourlyForecastView

This `WeatherHourlyForecastView` view is a horizontal scrollView that contains seven cells:

```
class WeatherHourlyForecastView: UIView {
    private var didSetupConstraints = false
    private let scrollView = UIScrollView()
    private var forecastCells = Array<WeatherHourForecastView>()

    override init(frame: CGRect) {
        super.init(frame: frame)
        setup()
        style()
    }

    required init(coder aDecoder: NSCoder) {
        fatalError("init(coder:) has not been implemented")
    }
    override func updateConstraints() {
        if didSetupConstraints {
            super.updateConstraints()
            return
        }
        layoutView()
```

```
        super.updateConstraints()
        didSetupConstraints = true
    }
}
```

The public part doesn't present anything new:

```
// MARK: Setup
private extension WeatherHourlyForecastView{
    func setup(){
        for i in 0..<7 {
            let cell = WeatherHourForecastView(frame: CGRectZero)
            forecastCells.append(cell)
            scrollView.addSubview(cell)
        }
        scrollView.showsHorizontalScrollIndicator = false
        addSubview(scrollView)
    }
}
```

The `setup()` function creates the cells and adds them to the scrollView.

We are saving the cells in an array too, in order to reference them later.

I could have used the subviews of the scrollView instead of using another variable, but I don't like to mix presentation with business logic. It hides the intentions of the programmer:

```
func layoutView(){
    layout(self) { view in
        view.height == 100
    }
    layout(scrollView) { view in
        view.top == view.superview!.top
        view.bottom == view.superview!.bottom
        view.left == view.superview!.left
        view.right == view.superview!.right
    }

    layout(forecastCells.first!) { view in
        view.left == view.superview!.left
    }
    layout(forecastCells.last!) { view in
        view.right == view.superview!.right
    }
```

```
        for idx in 1..<forecastCells.count {
            let previousCell = forecastCells[idx-1]
            let cell = forecastCells[idx]
            layout(previousCell, cell) { view, view2 in
                view.right == view2.left + 5
            }
        }
        for cell in forecastCells {
            layout(cell) { view in
                view.width == view.height
                view.height == view.superview!.height
                view.top == view.superview!.top
            }
        }
    }
```

The `layout()` function stacks the cells horizontally:

```
// MARK: Render
extension WeatherHourlyForecastView{
    func render(){
        for view in forecastCells {
            view.render()
        }
    }
}
```

The `render()` function just calls the render of the cells. Before implementing the cell, we must not forget to remove the color set for the background:

```
func style(){
}
```

Then, add the render calls to `PrettyWeatherViewController`:

```
func renderSubviews() {
    currentWeatherView.render()
    hourlyForecastView.render()
}
```

Moving on to `WeatherHourForecastView`:

```
import Cartography
import WeatherIconsKit

class WeatherHourForecastView: UIView {
    private var didSetupConstraints = false
```

```
    private let iconLabel = UILabel()
    private let hourLabel = UILabel()
    private let tempsLabel = UILabel()

    override init(frame: CGRect) {
        super.init(frame: frame)
        setup()
        style()
    }

    required init(coder aDecoder: NSCoder) {
        fatalError("init(coder:) has not been implemented")
    }
    override func updateConstraints() {
        if didSetupConstraints {
            super.updateConstraints()
            return
        }
        layoutView()
        super.updateConstraints()
        didSetupConstraints = true
    }
}
```

We create three labels:

```
// MARK: Setup
private extension WeatherHourForecastView{
    func setup(){
        addSubview(iconLabel)
        addSubview(hourLabel)
        addSubview(tempsLabel)
    }
}

// MARK: Layout
private extension WeatherHourForecastView{
    func layoutView() {
        layout(iconLabel) { view in
            view.center == view.superview!.center
            view.height == 50
        }
        layout(hourLabel) { view in
            view.centerX == view.superview!.centerX
            view.top == view.superview!.top
```

```
        }
        layout(tempsLabel) { view in
            view.centerX == view.superview!.centerX
            view.bottom == view.superview!.bottom
        }
    }
}
```

After adding them to the view, we set them like this: one at the top, the second in the center, and the last at the bottom:

```
// MARK: Style
private extension WeatherHourForecastView{
    func style(){
        iconLabel.textColor = UIColor.whiteColor()
        hourLabel.font = UIFont.latoFontOfSize(20)
        hourLabel.textColor = UIColor.whiteColor()
        tempsLabel.font = UIFont.latoFontOfSize(20)
        tempsLabel.textColor = UIColor.whiteColor()
    }
}


// MARK: Render
extension WeatherHourForecastView{
    func render(){
        var dateFormatter = NSDateFormatter()
        dateFormatter.dateFormat = "HH:mm"
        hourLabel.text = dateFormatter.stringFromDate(NSDate())
        iconLabel.attributedText = WIKFontIcon.
wiDaySunnyIconWithSize(30).attributedString()

        tempsLabel.text = "5° 8°"
    }
}
```

When run at this stage, the app starts looking gorgeous!

WeatherDaysForecastView

The WeatherDaysForecastView view is pretty similar to WeatherHourForecastView; the only difference is that the cells are stacked vertically, not horizontally:

```
        private var forecastCells = Array<WeatherDayForecastView>()
```

Again, we add an array with the cells:

```
func setup(){
    for i in 0..<7 {
        let cell = WeatherDayForecastView(frame: CGRectZero)
        forecastCells.append(cell)
        addSubview(cell)
    }
}
```

We create them and add them to the view and the internal array:

```
// MARK: Layout
private extension WeatherDaysForecastView{
    func layoutView(){
        setTranslatesAutoresizingMaskIntoConstraints(false)
        layout(forecastCells.first!) { view in
            view.top == view.superview!.top
        }

        for idx in 1..<forecastCells.count {
            let previousCell = forecastCells[idx-1]
            let cell = forecastCells[idx]
            layout(cell, previousCell) { view, view2 in
                view.top == view2.bottom
            }
        }
        for cell in forecastCells {
            layout(cell) { view in
                view.left == view.superview!.left
                view.right == view.superview!.right
            }
        }
        layout(forecastCells.last!) { view in
            view.bottom == view.superview!.bottom
        }
    }
}
```

We lay them out, paying attention to disable the translation from the autoresizingMask to AutoLayout constraints for the view itself. Cartography disables it, but in this case, we set constraints only on the subviews, leaving the view without explicit constraints at this level:

```
// MARK: Render
extension WeatherDaysForecastView{
    func render(){
        for view in forecastCells {
            view.render()
```

```
            }
        }
    }
```

Again, the render only forwards functions. We remove the set of the background color:

```
// MARK: Style
private extension WeatherDaysForecastView{
    func style(){
    }
}
```

We add the render method to `PrettyWeatherViewController`:

```
func renderSubviews() {
    currentWeatherView.render()
    hourlyForecastView.render()
    daysForecastView.render()
}
```

The `WeatherDayForecast` class is similar to `WeatherHourForecastView`:

```
import Foundation
import Cartography
import WeatherIconsKit

class WeatherDayForecastView: UIView {
    private var didSetupConstraints = false
    private let iconLabel = UILabel()
    private let dayLabel = UILabel()
    private let tempsLabel = UILabel()

    override init(frame: CGRect) {
        super.init(frame: frame)
        setup()
        style()
    }

    required init(coder aDecoder: NSCoder) {
        fatalError("init(coder:) has not been implemented")
    }
    override func updateConstraints() {
        if didSetupConstraints {
            super.updateConstraints()
            return
        }
```

```
            layoutView()
            super.updateConstraints()
            didSetupConstraints = true
        }
    }
```

We add the labels:

```
    // MARK: Setup
    private extension WeatherDayForecastView{
        func setup(){
            addSubview(dayLabel)
            addSubview(iconLabel)
            addSubview(tempsLabel)
        }
    }


    // MARK: Layout
    private extension WeatherDayForecastView{
        func layoutView() {
            layout(self) { view in
                view.height == 50
            }

            layout(iconLabel) { view in
                view.centerY == view.superview!.centerY
                view.left == view.superview!.left + 20
                view.width == view.height
                view.height == 50
            }

            layout(dayLabel, iconLabel) { view, view2 in
                view.centerY == view.superview!.centerY
                view.left == view2.right + 20
            }

            layout(tempsLabel) { view in
                view.centerY == view.superview!.centerY
                view.right == view.superview!.right - 20
            }
        }
    }
```

As usual, the layout part is long, but straightforward:

```
// MARK: Style
private extension WeatherDayForecastView{
    func style(){
        iconLabel.textColor = UIColor.whiteColor()
        dayLabel.font = UIFont.latoFontOfSize(20)
        dayLabel.textColor = UIColor.whiteColor()
        tempsLabel.font = UIFont.latoFontOfSize(20)
        tempsLabel.textColor = UIColor.whiteColor()
    }
}


// MARK: Render
extension WeatherDayForecastView{
    func render(){
        var dateFormatter = NSDateFormatter()
        dateFormatter.dateFormat = "EEEE"
        dayLabel.text = dateFormatter.stringFromDate(NSDate())
        iconLabel.attributedText = WIKFontIcon.
wiDaySunnyIconWithSize(30).attributedString()

        tempsLabel.text = "7°     11°"
    }
}
```

Now, run the app; it is really gorgeous!

The only thing missing from a UI point of view is to blur the background when the scrollView reaches the bottom.

Blurring the background

The first naïve idea would be to change the level of blurriness depending on the position of the scrollView, but it will be really inefficient because the blur operation is CPU intensive, and it won't be smooth on older devices.

So, the idea is to trick the user. Instead of blurring the image at every change of position of the scrollView, we blur the image, only before setting it to the UIImageView. Then, we set the alpha channel to 0 (which means transparent). Next, we change the alpha depending on the position, reaching the opaque when the scrollView offset reaches half.

First of all, we need to import the framework to blur the image:

```
import FXBlurView
```

Then, create the overlay view and set as subview:

```
private let overlayView = UIImageView()
//...
func setup(){
    //...
    overlayView.contentMode = .ScaleAspectFill
    overlayView.clipsToBounds = true
  view.addSubview(overlayView)
    //...
    scrollView.delegate = self
    view.addSubview(scrollView)
}
func layoutView() {
    //...
    layout(overlayView) { view in
        view.top == view.superview!.top
        view.bottom == view.superview!.bottom
        view.left == view.superview!.left
        view.right == view.superview!.right
    }
```

Next, in the `render()` function, we set the blurred image:

```
func render(image: UIImage?){
    if let image = image {
        backgroundView.image = image
        overlayView.image = image.blurredImageWithRadius(10,
iterations: 20, tintColor: UIColor.clearColor())
        overlayView.alpha = 0
    }
}
```

Note that we set the image as transparent.

I believe you've noticed that we set the ViewController as a delegate of the `scrollView`. This allows us to detect the change in position during scrolling:

```
// MARK: UIScrollViewDelegate
extension PrettyWeatherViewController: UIScrollViewDelegate{
    func scrollViewDidScroll(scrollView: UIScrollView) {
        let offset = scrollView.contentOffset.y
        let treshold: CGFloat = CGFloat(view.frame.height)/2
        overlayView.alpha = min(1.0, offset/treshold)

    }
}
```

As you can see, the code is straightforward—we set the alpha channel to be proportional to the position. Now, by running the app, we can see how good it looks:

 You can find the code for this version at `https://github.com/gscalzo/PrettyWeather/tree/UI_done`.

Downloading the background image

Before moving on to download the actual forecast, we'll introduce the topic of networking downloading a geolocalized background image.

Searching in Flickr

To get an image, we'll use the API of Flickr, a famous image-hosting website. First of all, we override the `viewWillAppear` function in `PrettyWeatherApp` so that a new image will be downloaded every time the ViewController appears:

```
override func viewWillAppear(animated: Bool) {
    super.viewWillAppear(animated)

    let lat:Double = 48.8567
    let lon:Double = 2.3508

    FlickrDatastore().retrieveImageAtLat(lat, lon: lon){ image in
        self.render(image)
    }
}
```

To implement the searching feature, we set a dummy value using the coordinates of Paris. Then, we create a new file named `FlickrDatastore`:

```
import FlickrKit

class FlickrDatastore {
    private let OBJECTIVE_FLICKR_API_KEY = "CREATE_API_KEY"
    private let OBJECTIVE_FLICKR_API_SHARED_SECRET = "CREATE_SHARED_
SECRET"
    private let GROUP_ID = "1463451@N25"

    func retrieveImageAtLat(lat: Double, lon: Double, closure: (image:
UIImage?) -> Void){
    }

    private func extractImageFk(fk: FlickrKit, response: AnyObject?,
        error: NSError?, closure: (image: UIImage?) -> Void) {
    }
}
```

To use the Flickr API, you need to request an API key and a secret key. These can be requested for free after logging in.

The api key can be requested at `https://www.flickr.com/services/apps/create/`.

To get images that are suitable for our app, we select pictures from a group where users upload images related to the weather:

```
func retrieveImageAtLat(lat: Double, lon: Double, closure: (image:
UIImage?) -> Void){
    let fk = FlickrKit.sharedFlickrKit()
    fk.initializeWithAPIKey(OBJECTIVE_FLICKR_API_KEY,
sharedSecret: OBJECTIVE_FLICKR_API_SHARED_SECRET)

    fk.call("flickr.photos.search", args: [
        "group_id": GROUP_ID,
        "lat": "\(lat)",
        "lon": "\(lon)",
        "radius": "10"
        ], maxCacheAge: FKDUMaxAgeOneHour) { (response, error) ->
Void in
            self.extractImageFk(fk, response: response,
                error: error,
                closure: closure)
    }
}
```

As you can see, using `FlickrKit` is really straightforward.

However, the result is a JSON string, and parsing a JSON string in Swift is not as simple as it is in Objective-C.

The reasons for this lie in the heterogeneity of the result. This means that JSON can contain different types, whereas Swift pushes for the homogeneity of containers, and the intrinsic optionality of the dictionary as a container, which means that we need to check the existence of every value we are getting from a dictionary.

The implementation of `extractImage()` will explain the problem better:

```
private func extractImageFk(fk: FlickrKit, response: AnyObject?,
    error: NSError?, closure: (image: UIImage?) -> Void) {
    if let response = response as? [String:AnyObject]{
        if let photos = response["photos"] as? [String:AnyObject]
{
            if let listOfPhotos: AnyObject = photos["photo"] {
                if listOfPhotos.count > 0 {
                    let randomIndex = Int(arc4random_
uniform(UInt32(listOfPhotos.count)))
                    let photo = listOfPhotos[randomIndex] as!
[String:AnyObject]
                    let url = fk.photoURLForSize(FKPhotoSizeMedi
um640,
```

```
                              fromPhotoDictionary: photo)
                    let image = UIImage(data:
    NSData(contentsOfURL: url)!)
                       dispatch_async(dispatch_get_main_queue()){
                          closure(image: image!)
                       }
                    }
                 }
              }
           } else {
              println(error)
              println(response)
           }
        }
```

The format of the JSON returned is as follows:

```
{photos: {
     page: 1,
     pages: 3,
     perpage: 250,
     photo: [
              {
                farm = 8,
                id = 16172607518,
                ...
              },
              {
                farm = 2,
                id = 16132447518,
                ...
              },
              ...
           ]
     }
}
```

We need the array of photo. This can be reached by accessing two nested dictionaries, and because every access to a value using a key is optional, we need to verify that the values is not nil and creating this unpleasant cascade effect.

When we get the array, we extract a random element and download the image.

Because the response from the server runs in a background thread, it is safe to download the image synchronously without fearing to freeze the UI.

As you can imagine, the nested conditions lead to poor readability of the code, but after Swift 1.2, released in Xcode 8.3, Apple made optional unwrapping with `if let` more powerful. This allows you to unwrap more optionals in the same condition, and you can also add logical conditions to the same `if` block using the `where` keyword.

Hence, the previous code can be written in more concise way like this:

```
if let response = response as? [String:AnyObject],
    photos = response["photos"] as? [String:AnyObject],
    listOfPhotos: AnyObject = photos["photo"]
    where listOfPhotos.count > 0 {
        //...
} else {
    println(error)
    println(response)
}
```

By running the app, we get random images of Paris.

 This code can be found at `https://github.com/gscalzo/PrettyWeather/tree/download_image`.

Geolocalising the app

As a test, we have used dummy coordinates, but we do have a powerful GPS on board, and it's time to use it.

Using CoreLocation

To use the location service, we need to instruct iOS that our app is using it.

To do this, we must add the `NSLocationAlwaysUsageDescription` key with a string, for example, "This application requires location services to get the weather of your current location." in `Info.plist`.

Then, we add a new property to `PrettyWeatherViewController`:

```
private var locationDatastore: LocationDatastore?
```

Next, we change the `viewWillAppear` function:

```
    override func viewWillAppear(animated: Bool) {
        super.viewWillAppear(animated)
        locationDatastore = LocationDatastore() { [weak self] location
in
            FlickrDatastore().retrieveImageAtLat(location.lat, lon:
location.lon){ image in
                self?.render(image)
                return
            }
        }
    }
```

Our simple wrapper around `LocationManager` basically calls the provided closure when the location changes. The implementation is straightforward:

```
import CoreLocation

struct Location {
    let lat: Double
    let lon: Double
}

class LocationDatastore: NSObject, CLLocationManagerDelegate {
    private let locationManager = CLLocationManager()

    typealias LocationClosure = (Location) -> Void
    private let onLocationFound: LocationClosure

    init(closure: LocationClosure){
        onLocationFound = closure
        super.init()
        locationManager.delegate = self
        locationManager.requestAlwaysAuthorization()
        startUpdating()
    }


    private func startUpdating() {
        locationManager.startUpdatingLocation()
    }

    private func stopUpdating() {
        locationManager.stopUpdatingLocation()
```

```
        }

    func locationManager(manager: CLLocationManager!, didFailWithError
error: NSError!) {
        locationManager.stopUpdatingLocation()
        NSLog("Error: \(error)")
        dispatch_async(dispatch_get_main_queue()){
            self.onLocationFound(Location(lat: 37.3175, lon:
122.0419))
        }
    }

    func locationManager(manager: CLLocationManager!,
didUpdateLocations locations: [AnyObject]) {
        var locationArray = locations as NSArray
        var locationObj = locationArray.lastObject as! CLLocation
        var coord = locationObj.coordinate

        dispatch_async(dispatch_get_main_queue()){
            self.onLocationFound(Location(lat: coord.latitude, lon:
coord.longitude))
        }

        stopUpdating()
    }

    func locationManager(manager: CLLocationManager!,
        didChangeAuthorizationStatus status: CLAuthorizationStatus) {
            switch status {
            case .Restricted:
                NSLog("Denied access: Restricted Access to location")
            case .Denied:
                NSLog("Denied access: User denied access to location")
            case .NotDetermined:
                NSLog("Denied access: Status not determined")
            default:
                NSLog("Allowed to location Access")
                startUpdating()
            }
    }
}
```

If you run the app now, a popup asking for permission to use the location services appears. If you deny the permission, to simplify the error handling, hardcoded coordinates are passed.

 You can find the code for this version at https://github.com/ gscalzo/PrettyWeather/tree/geolocalisation.

Retrieving the actual forecast

We have almost completed the app, but it is still missing the most important part—the weather forecast.

Getting the forecast from OpenWeatherMap

There are a plenty of services that provide forecast for free or for a small amount of money.

For our app, we'll use `http://openweathermap.org`, whose API is free for a small number of calls.

First of all, we create the struct to handle the forecast:

```
import Foundation
struct WeatherCondition {
    let cityName: String?
    let weather: String
    let icon: IconType?
    let time: NSDate
    let tempKelvin: Double
    let maxTempKelvin: Double
    let minTempKelvin: Double

    var tempFahrenheit: Double {
        get {
            return tempCelsius * 9.0/5.0 + 32.0
        }
    }

    var maxTempFahrenheit: Double {
        get {
            return maxTempCelsius * 9.0/5.0 + 32.0
        }
    }
    var minTempFahrenheit: Double {
        get {
            return minTempCelsius * 9.0/5.0 + 32.0
        }
    }

    var tempCelsius: Double {
        get {
            return tempKelvin - 273.15
        }
    }
    var maxTempCelsius: Double {
        get {
            return maxTempKelvin - 273.15
        }
    }
    var minTempCelsius: Double {
        get {
            return minTempKelvin - 273.15
        }
    }
}
```

Because the service returns the temperature in Kelvin, we provide the computed properties to get the temperature in either degrees Celsius or degrees Fahrenheit.

The `IconType` enumeration is just an enumeration of the possible icons returned from the server:

```
enum IconType: String {
    case i01d = "01d"
    case i01n = "01n"
    case i02d = "02d"
    case i02n = "02n"
    case i03d = "03d"
    case i03n = "03n"
    case i04d = "04d"
    case i04n = "04n"
    case i09d = "09d"
    case i09n = "09n"
    case i10d = "10d"
    case i10n = "10n"
    case i11d = "11d"
    case i11n = "11n"
    case i13d = "13d"
    case i13n = "13n"
    case i50d = "50d"
    case i50n = "50n"
}
```

 The possible codes for the forecast can be seen at `http://openweathermap.org/weather-conditions`.

Then, we change the `viewWillAppear` function in `PrettyWeatherViewController` again. We do this to raise three calls to get the current weather and the forecast:

```
override func viewWillAppear(animated: Bool) {
    super.viewWillAppear(animated)
    locationDatastore = LocationDatastore() { [weak self] location
in
        FlickrDatastore().retrieveImageAtLat(location.lat, lon:
location.lon){ image in
            self?.render(image)
            return
        }
        let weatherDatastore = WeatherDatastore()
```

```
        weatherDatastore.retrieveCurrentWeatherAtLat(location.lat,
lon: location.lon) {
            currentWeatherConditions in
            self?.renderCurrent(currentWeatherConditions)
            return
        }
        weatherDatastore.retrieveHourlyForecastAtLat(location.lat,
lon: location.lon) {
            hourlyWeatherConditions in
            self?.renderHourly(hourlyWeatherConditions)
            return
        }
        weatherDatastore.retrieveDailyForecastAtLat(location.lat,
lon: location.lon, dayCnt: 7) {
            hourlyWeatherConditions in
            self?.renderDaily(hourlyWeatherConditions)
            return
        }
    }
}
```

The renders are just functions used to forward the requests to the subviews:

```
func renderCurrent(currentWeatherConditions: WeatherCondition){
    currentWeatherView.render(currentWeatherConditions)
}

func renderHourly(weatherConditions: Array<WeatherCondition>){
    hourlyForecastView.render(weatherConditions)
}

func renderDaily(weatherConditions: Array<WeatherCondition>){
    daysForecastView.render(weatherConditions)
}
```

Don't forget to remove `renderSubviews()`.

Rendering CurrentWeatherView

After removing the dummy `render()` function, we add this function:

```
func render(weatherCondition: WeatherCondition){
    iconLbl.attributedText = iconStringFromIcon(weatherCondition.
icon!, 20)
    weatherLbl.text = weatherCondition.weather
```

```
        var usesMetric = false
        if let localeSystem = NSLocale.currentLocale().objectForKey(NS
LocaleUsesMetricSystem) as? Bool {
            usesMetric = localeSystem
        }

        if usesMetric {
            minTempLbl.text = "\(weatherCondition.minTempCelsius.
roundToInt())°"
            maxTempLbl.text = "\(weatherCondition.maxTempCelsius.
roundToInt())°"
            currentTempLbl.text = "\(weatherCondition.tempCelsius.
roundToInt())°"
        } else {
            minTempLbl.text = "\(weatherCondition.minTempFahrenheit.
roundToInt())°"
            maxTempLbl.text = "\(weatherCondition.maxTempFahrenheit.
roundToInt())°"
            currentTempLbl.text = "\(weatherCondition.tempFahrenheit.
roundToInt())°"
        }

        cityLbl.text = weatherCondition.cityName ?? ""
    }
```

Because we want to represent the temperature as an integer, and not as a double, we have created a convenience category to `double`:

```
extension Double {
    func roundToInt() -> Int{
        return Int(round(self))
    }
}
```

Also, we have added a function to convert `IconType` to an icon in `WeatherIconsKit`:

```
import WeatherIconsKit

func iconStringFromIcon(icon: IconType, size: CGFloat) ->
NSAttributedString {
    switch icon {
    case .i01d:
        return WIKFontIcon.wiDaySunnyIconWithSize(size).
attributedString()
    case .i01n:
        return WIKFontIcon.wiNightClearIconWithSize(size).
attributedString()
```

```
        case .i02d:
            return WIKFontIcon.wiDayCloudyIconWithSize(size).
attributedString()
        case .i02n:
            return WIKFontIcon.wiNightCloudyIconWithSize(size).
attributedString()
        case .i03d:
            return WIKFontIcon.wiDayCloudyIconWithSize(size).
attributedString()
        case .i03n:
            return WIKFontIcon.wiNightCloudyIconWithSize(size).
attributedString()
        case .i04d:
            return WIKFontIcon.wiCloudyIconWithSize(size).
attributedString()
        case .i04n:
            return WIKFontIcon.wiCloudyIconWithSize(size).
attributedString()
        case .i09d:
            return WIKFontIcon.wiDayShowersIconWithSize(size).
attributedString()
        case .i09n:
            return WIKFontIcon.wiNightShowersIconWithSize(size).
attributedString()
        case .i10d:
            return WIKFontIcon.wiDayRainIconWithSize(size).
attributedString()
        case .i10n:
            return WIKFontIcon.wiNightRainIconWithSize(size).
attributedString()
        case .i11d:
            return WIKFontIcon.wiDayThunderstormIconWithSize(size).
attributedString()
        case .i11n:
            return WIKFontIcon.wiNightThunderstormIconWithSize(size).
attributedString()
        case .i13d:
            return WIKFontIcon.wiSnowIconWithSize(size).attributedString()
        case .i13n:
            return WIKFontIcon.wiSnowIconWithSize(size).attributedString()
        case .i50d:
            return WIKFontIcon.wiFogIconWithSize(size).attributedString()
        case .i50n:
            return WIKFontIcon.wiFogIconWithSize(size).attributedString()
        }
    }
```

Rendering WeatherHourlyForecastView

The render function just iterates through all the subviews and calls `render()`:

```
// MARK: Render
extension WeatherHourlyForecastView{
    func render(weatherConditions: Array<WeatherCondition>){
        for (idx, view) in enumerate(forecastCells) {
            view.render(weatherConditions[idx])
        }
    }
}
```

In WeatherHourForecastView we use the same approach we used for the current weather: // MARK: Render
extension WeatherHourForecastView{

```
    func render(weatherCondition: WeatherCondition){
        var dateFormatter = NSDateFormatter()
        dateFormatter.dateFormat = "HH:mm"
        hourLabel.text = dateFormatter.
stringFromDate(weatherCondition.time)
        iconLabel.attributedText = iconStringFromIcon(weatherConditi
on.icon!, 30)

        var usesMetric = false
        if let localeSystem = NSLocale.currentLocale().objectForKey(NS
LocaleUsesMetricSystem) as? Bool {
            usesMetric = localeSystem
        }

        if usesMetric {
            tempsLabel.text = "\(weatherCondition.minTempCelsius.
roundToInt())° \(weatherCondition.maxTempCelsius.roundToInt())°"
        } else {
            tempsLabel.text = "\(weatherCondition.minTempFahrenheit.
roundToInt())° \(weatherCondition.maxTempFahrenheit.roundToInt())°"
        }
    }
}
```

Rendering WeatherDaysForecastView

Even in this case, the flow is exactly the same. First, we iterate to forward the call to the subviews:

```
extension WeatherDaysForecastView{
    func render(weatherConditions: Array<WeatherCondition>){
        for (idx, view) in enumerate(forecastCells) {
            view.render(weatherConditions[idx])
        }
    }
}
```

Then, in `WeatherDayForecast`, we render the weather condition:

```
// MARK: Render
extension WeatherDayForecastView{
    func render(weatherCondition: WeatherCondition){
        var dateFormatter = NSDateFormatter()
        dateFormatter.dateFormat = "EEEE"
        dayLabel.text = dateFormatter.stringFromDate(weatherCondition.
time)
        iconLabel.attributedText = iconStringFromIcon(weatherConditi
on.icon!, 30)

        var usesMetric = false
        if let localeSystem = NSLocale.currentLocale().objectForKey(NS
LocaleUsesMetricSystem) as? Bool {
            usesMetric = localeSystem
        }

        if usesMetric {
            tempsLabel.text = "\(weatherCondition.minTempCelsius.
roundToInt())°    \(weatherCondition.maxTempCelsius.roundToInt())°"
        } else {
            tempsLabel.text = "\(weatherCondition.minTempFahrenheit.
roundToInt())°    \(weatherCondition.maxTempFahrenheit.
roundToInt())°"
        }
    }
}
```

Connecting to the server

This class uses Alamofire, the Swift equivalent of AFNetworking, the most used third-party library to help handle network communications in iOS. This class also uses SwiftyJson, which eliminates the problem of the nested checks for optionals during the decoding of **JSON** (short for **JavaScript Object Notation**, a lightweight data interchange format) data:

```
import Foundation
import CoreLocation
import Alamofire
import SwiftyJSON

class WeatherDatastore {
    func retrieveCurrentWeatherAtLat(lat: CLLocationDegrees, lon:
CLLocationDegrees,
        block: (weatherCondition: WeatherCondition) -> Void) {
    }

    func retrieveHourlyForecastAtLat(lat: CLLocationDegrees,
        lon: CLLocationDegrees,
        block: (weatherConditions: Array<WeatherCondition>) -> Void) {
    }

    func retrieveDailyForecastAtLat(lat: Double,
        lon: Double,
        dayCnt: Int,
        block: (weatherConditions: Array<WeatherCondition>) -> Void) {
    }

}
```

The first method asks for the current weather and parses the JSON response to convert to our struct:

```
    func retrieveCurrentWeatherAtLat(lat: CLLocationDegrees, lon:
CLLocationDegrees,
        block: (weatherCondition: WeatherCondition) -> Void) {
            let url = "http://api.openweathermap.org/data/2.5/weather"
            let params = ["lat":lat, "lon":lon]

            Alamofire.request(.GET, url, parameters: params)
                .responseJSON { (request, response, json, error) in
                    println(response)
                    if(error != nil || json == nil) {
```

```
                              println("Error: \(error)")
                } else {
                    let json = JSON(json!)
                    block(weatherCondition: self.createWeatherCond
    itionFronJson(json))
                }
            }
        }
```

The `createWeatherConditionFromJson()` function is responsible for the conversion:

```
    private extension WeatherDatastore {
        func createWeatherConditionFronJson(json: JSON) ->
    WeatherCondition{
            let name = json["name"].string
            let weather = json["weather"][0]["main"].stringValue
            let icon = json["weather"][0]["icon"].stringValue
            let dt = json["dt"].doubleValue
            let time = NSDate(timeIntervalSince1970: dt)
            let tempKelvin = json["main"]["temp"].doubleValue
            let maxTempKelvin = json["main"]["temp_max"].doubleValue
            let minTempKelvin = json["main"]["temp_min"].doubleValue

            return WeatherCondition(
                cityName: name,
                weather: weather,
                icon: IconType(rawValue: icon),
                time: time,
                tempKelvin: tempKelvin,
                maxTempKelvin: maxTempKelvin,
                minTempKelvin: minTempKelvin)
        }
    }
```

Here, as we can see, SwiftyJson permits us to write denser code because the SwiftJson dictionary handles the optional result in clever way — using internal optional chaining, the expression returns `nil` if any of its components returns nil.

The `retrieveHourlyForecast()` function is basically the same as the current weather; the only difference is that it returns an array of `WeatherCondition`:

```
    func retrieveHourlyForecastAtLat(lat: CLLocationDegrees,
        lon: CLLocationDegrees,
        block: (weatherConditions: Array<WeatherCondition>) -> Void) {
```

```
                let url = "http://api.openweathermap.org/data/2.5/
forecast"
                let params = ["lat":lat, "lon":lon]
                Alamofire.request(.GET, url, parameters: params)
                    .responseJSON { (request, response, json, error) in
                        if(error != nil || json == nil) {
                            println("Error: \(error)")
                        }
                        else {
                            let json = JSON(json!)
                            let list: Array<JSON> = json["list"].
arrayValue

                            let weatherConditions: Array<WeatherCondition>
= list.map() {
                                return self.
createWeatherConditionFronJson($0)
                            }
                            block(weatherConditions: weatherConditions)
                        }
                }
        }
```

Finally, retrieveDailyForecast() returns an array for the forecast of the upcoming days. Note that OpenWeatherMap returns an array of days that contains the actual day as well, so we need to get rid of the first element:

```
func retrieveDailyForecastAtLat(lat: Double,
        lon: Double,
        dayCnt: Int,
        block: (weatherConditions: Array<WeatherCondition>) -> Void) {
            let url = "http://api.openweathermap.org/data/2.5/
forecast/daily"
                let params = ["lat":lat, "lon":lon,
"cnt":Double(dayCnt+1)]
                Alamofire.request(.GET, url, parameters: params)
                    .responseJSON { (request, response, json, error) in
                        if(error != nil || json == nil) {
                            println("Error: \(error)")
                        } else {
                            var json = JSON(json!)
                            let list: Array<JSON> = json["list"].
arrayValue

                            let weatherConditions: Array<WeatherCondition>
= list.map() {
```

```
                                return self.createDayForecastFronJson($0)
                            }
                            let count = weatherConditions.count
                            let daysWithoutToday = Array(weatherCondition
      s[1..<count])

                            block(weatherConditions: daysWithoutToday)
                        }
                    }
                }
```

Unfortunately, the format of the response is a little different from the responses to the former requests; hence, we need to build a new conversion function:

```
func createDayForecastFronJson(json: JSON) -> WeatherCondition{
    let name = ""
    let weather = json["weather"][0]["main"].stringValue
    let icon = json["weather"][0]["icon"].stringValue
    let dt = json["dt"].doubleValue
    let time = NSDate(timeIntervalSince1970: dt)
    let tempKelvin = json["temp"]["day"].doubleValue
    let maxTempKelvin = json["temp"]["max"].doubleValue
    let minTempKelvin = json["temp"]["min"].doubleValue

    return WeatherCondition(
        cityName: name,
        weather: weather,
        icon: IconType(rawValue: icon),
        time: time,
        tempKelvin: tempKelvin,
        maxTempKelvin: maxTempKelvin,
        minTempKelvin: minTempKelvin)

}
```

And, with this, our pretty weather app is done! The following screenshot shows how the app will look:

 You can find the code for this version at https://github.com/
gscalzo/PrettyWeather/tree/app_is_done.

Where do we go from here?

Although our app is almost complete, the possibilities for expanding it are endless.

Starting from this source, you can do the following:

- Make it more robust in handling error situations. Currently, if anything goes wrong, nothing happens on the user's side because the app just logs the error. A good strategy would be to present a warning somewhere and give the chance to retry the operation to the user.

- The app works well if the user allows the use of GPS, but it will stop working if the user denies it. How about adding a functionality to see the weather for more cities than one, swiping horizontally to see a new city?

- In the app, the background is chosen using only coordinates, but because the images in that group are tagged with the weather, it would be nice to show an image that matches the weather, and, maybe, with the correct time of the day or night.

- A straightforward but really useful feature would be to add the pull-to-refresh functionality to request the weather again.

- We presented a minimal amount of data. OpenWeatherMap offers more data, and it can be presented in a nice way.

- To verify that the separation layers are solid, it would be interesting to add the chance to use a different weather provider (that is, Weather Underground or forecast.io), and to ensure that we don't need to change anything outside the data store.

Summary

This was a long chapter, again, full of information and firsthand experience.

We consolidated our architecture of classes, and the way in which we build the UI. You have finally learned how to connect to a server and how the option cascade chain can be solved.

After having implemented two utility apps, in the next couple of chapters, we are going to implement a game again. It is one of the most iconic games in recent years — *Flappy Bird*.

5
Flappy Swift

After having explored how to build *normal apps* with the last two apps, let's go back to games.

These apps will use two useful frameworks that iOS provides for casual game developers — SKSprite and SKScene. The former is a handy and powerful 2D game framework that provides a physics engine based on Box2D. The latter allows indie game developers to implement three-dimensional games.

Let's start using the first framework by implementing a nice clone of *Flappy Bird*.

The app is…

Only someone who has been living under a rock for the past two years may not have heard of Flappy Bird, but to be sure that everybody understands the game, let's go through a brief introduction.

Flappy Bird is a simple, but addictive, game where the player controls a bird that must fly between a series of pipes. Gravity pulls the bird down, but by touching the screen, the player can make the bird flap and move towards the sky, driving the bird through a gap in a couple of pipes. The goal is to pass through as many pipes as possible.

Our implementation will be a high-fidelity tribute to the original game, with the same simplicity and difficulty level. The app will consist of only two screens—a clean menu screen and the game itself—as shown in the following screenshot:

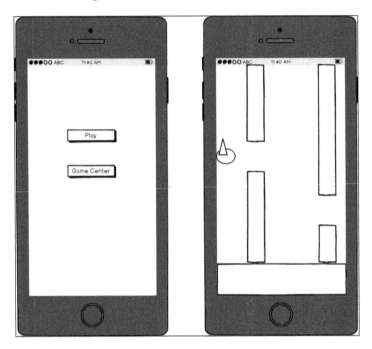

Building the skeleton of the app

Let's start implementing the skeleton of our game using the SpriteKit game template.

Creating the project

For implementing a SpriteKit game, Xcode provides a convenient template, which prepares a project with all the useful settings:

1. Go to **New | Project** and select the **Game** template, as shown in this screenshot:

2. In the following screen, after filling in all the fields, pay attention and select **SpriteKit** under **Game Technology**, like this:

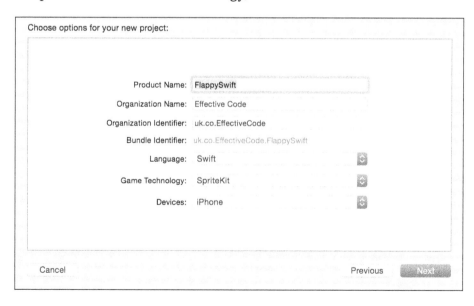

3. By running the app and touching the screen, you will be delighted by the cute, rotating airplanes!

Implementing the menu

First of all, let's add CocoaPods; write the following code in the Podfile:

```
use_frameworks!

target 'FlappySwift' do
  pod 'Cartography', '~> 0.5'
  pod 'HTPressableButton', '~> 1.3'
end
```

Then install CocoaPods by running the `pod install` command. As usual, we are going to implement the UI without using Interface Builder and the storyboards. Go to `AppDelegate` and add these lines to create the main ViewController:

```
    func application(application: UIApplication,
didFinishLaunchingWithOptions launchOptions: [NSObject: AnyObject]?)
-> Bool {
        let viewController = MenuViewController()
```

```
    let mainWindow = UIWindow(frame: UIScreen.mainScreen().bounds)
    mainWindow.backgroundColor = UIColor.whiteColor()
    mainWindow.rootViewController = viewController
    mainWindow.makeKeyAndVisible()
    window = mainWindow

    return true
}
```

The `MenuViewController`, as the name suggests, implements a nice menu to choose between the game and the Game Center, which we'll see in the next chapter:

```
import UIKit
import HTPressableButton
import Cartography

class MenuViewController: UIViewController {
    private let playButton = HTPressableButton(frame: CGRectMake(0, 0,
260, 50), buttonStyle: .Rect)
    private let gameCenterButton = HTPressableButton(frame:
CGRectMake(0, 0, 260, 50), buttonStyle: .Rect)

    override func viewDidLoad() {
        super.viewDidLoad()
        setup()
        layoutView()
        style()
        render()
    }
}
```

As you can see, we are using the usual structure. Just for the sake of making the UI prettier, we are using `HTPressableButtons` instead of the default buttons.

Despite the fact that we are using AutoLayout, the implementation of this custom button requires that we instantiate the button by passing a frame to it:

```
// MARK: Setup
private extension MenuViewController{
    func setup(){
        playButton.addTarget(self, action: "onPlayPressed:",
forControlEvents: .TouchUpInside)
        view.addSubview(playButton)
        gameCenterButton.addTarget(self, action:
"onGameCenterPressed:", forControlEvents: .TouchUpInside)
        view.addSubview(gameCenterButton)
```

```
    }

    @objc func onPlayPressed(sender: UIButton) {
        let vc = GameViewController()
        vc.modalTransitionStyle = .CrossDissolve
        presentViewController(vc, animated: true, completion: nil)
    }

    @objc func onGameCenterPressed(sender: UIButton) {
        println("onGameCenterPressed")
    }
}
```

The only thing to note is that, because we are setting the function to be called when the button is pressed using the addTarget() function, we must prefix the designed methods using @objc. Otherwise, it will be impossible for the Objective-C runtime to find the correct method when the button is pressed. This is because they are implemented in a private extension; of course, you can set the extension as internal or public and you won't need to prepend @objc to the functions:

```
// MARK: Layout
extension MenuViewController{
    func layoutView() {
        layout(playButton) { view in
            view.bottom == view.superview!.centerY - 60
            view.centerX == view.superview!.centerX
            view.height == 80
            view.width == view.superview!.width - 40
        }
        layout(gameCenterButton) { view in
            view.bottom == view.superview!.centerY + 60
            view.centerX == view.superview!.centerX
            view.height == 80
            view.width == view.superview!.width - 40
        }
    }
}
```

The layout functions simply put the two buttons in the correct places on the screen:

```
// MARK: Style
private extension MenuViewController{
    func style(){
        playButton.buttonColor = UIColor.ht_grapeFruitColor()
        playButton.shadowColor = UIColor.ht_grapeFruitDarkColor()
```

```
            gameCenterButton.buttonColor = UIColor.ht_aquaColor()
            gameCenterButton.shadowColor = UIColor.ht_aquaDarkColor()
        }
    }


    // MARK: Render
    private extension MenuViewController{
        func render(){
            playButton.setTitle("Play", forState: .Normal)
            gameCenterButton.setTitle("Game Center", forState: .Normal)
        }
    }
```

Finally, we set the colors and text for the titles of the buttons. The following screenshot shows the complete menu:

You will notice that on pressing **Play**, the app crashes. This is because the template is using the view defined in storyboard, and we are directly using the controllers.

Let's change the code in `GameViewController`:

```
class GameViewController: UIViewController {
    private let skView = SKView()

    override func viewDidLoad() {
        super.viewDidLoad()
        skView.frame = view.bounds
        view.addSubview(skView)
        if let scene = GameScene.unarchiveFromFile("GameScene") as?
GameScene {
            scene.size = skView.frame.size
            skView.showsFPS = true
            skView.showsNodeCount = true
            skView.ignoresSiblingOrder = true
            scene.scaleMode = .AspectFill
            skView.presentScene(scene)
        }
    }
}
```

We are basically creating the `SKView` programmatically, and setting its size just as we did for the main view's size.

If the app is run now, everything will work fine.

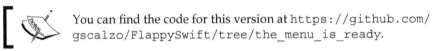

[You can find the code for this version at https://github.com/ gscalzo/FlappySwift/tree/the_menu_is_ready.]

A stage for a bird

Let's kick-start the game by implementing the background, which is not as straightforward as it might sound.

SpriteKit in a nutshell

SpriteKit is a powerful, but easy-to-use, game framework introduced in iOS 7.

It basically provides the infrastructure to move images onto the screen and interact with them.

It also provides a physics engine (based on Box2D), a particles engine, and basic sound playback support, making it particularly suitable for casual games.

The content of the game is drawn inside an SKView, which is a particular kind of UIView, so it can be placed inside a normal hierarchy of UIViews.

The content of the game is organized into scenes, represented by subclasses of SKScene. Different parts of the game, such as the menu, levels, and so on, must be implemented in different SKScenes. You can consider an SK in SpriteKit as an equivalent of the UIViewController.

Inside an SKScene, the elements of the game are grouped in the SKNode's tree which tells the SKScene how to render the components.

An SKNode can be either a drawable node, such as SKSpriteNode or SKShapeNode; or something to be applied to the subtree of its descendants, such as SKEffectNode or SKCropNode.

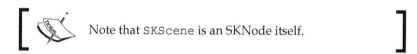 Note that SKScene is an SKNode itself.

Nodes are animated using SKAction.

An SKAction is a change that must be applied to a node, such as a move to a particular position, a change of scaling, or a change in the way the node appears. The actions can be grouped together to create actions that run in parallel, or wait for the end of a previous action.

Finally, we can define physics-based relations between objects, defining mass, gravity, and how the nodes interact with each other.

That said, the best way to understand and learn SpriteKit is by starting to play with it. So, without further ado, let's move on to the implementation of our tiny game. In this way, you'll get a complete understanding of the most important features of SpriteKit.

Explaining the code

In the previous section, we implemented the menu view, leaving the code similar to what was created by the template. With basic knowledge of SpriteKit, you can now start understanding the code:

```
class GameViewController: UIViewController {
    private let skView = SKView()

    override func viewDidLoad() {
        super.viewDidLoad()
        skView.frame = view.bounds
```

```
        view.addSubview(skView)
        if let scene = GameScene.unarchiveFromFile("GameScene") as?
GameScene {
            scene.size = skView.frame.size
            skView.showsFPS = true
            skView.showsNodeCount = true
            skView.ignoresSiblingOrder = true
            scene.scaleMode = .AspectFill
            skView.presentScene(scene)
        }
    }
}
```

This is the `UIViewController` that starts the game; it creates an `SKView` to present the full screen. Then it instantiates the scene from `GameScene.sks`, which can be considered the equivalent of a Storyboard. Next, it enables some debug information before presenting the scene.

It's now clear that we must implement the game inside the `GameScene` class.

Simulating a three-dimensional world using parallax

To simulate the depth of the in-game world, we are going to use the technique of parallax scrolling, a really popular method wherein the farther images on the game screen move slower than the closer images.

In our case, we have three different levels, and we'll use three different speeds:

Before implementing the scrolling background, we must import the images into our project, remembering to set each image as **2x** in the assets.

 The assets can be downloaded from `https://github.com/ gscalzo/FlappySwift/blob/master/assets.zip?raw=true`.

The `GameScene` class basically sets up the background levels:

```
import SpriteKit

class GameScene: SKScene {
    private var screenNode: SKSpriteNode!
    private var actors: [Startable]!

    override func didMoveToView(view: SKView) {
        screenNode = SKSpriteNode(color: UIColor.clearColor(), size:
self.size)
        addChild(screenNode)
        let sky = Background(textureNamed: "sky", duration:60.0).
addTo(screenNode)
        let city = Background(textureNamed: "city", duration:20.0).
addTo(screenNode)
        let ground = Background(textureNamed: "ground", duration:5.0).
addTo(screenNode)
        actors = [sky, city, ground]

        for actor in actors {
            actor.start()
        }
    }
}
```

The only implemented function is `didMoveToView()`, which can be considered the equivalent of `viewDidAppear` for a `UIVIewController`.

We define an array of `Startable` objects, where `Startable` is a protocol for making the life cycle of the scene, uniform:

```
import SpriteKit

protocol Startable {
    func start()
    func stop()
}
```

This will be handy for giving us an easy way to stop the game later, when either we reach the final goal or our character dies. The `Background` class holds the behavior for a scrollable level:

```
import SpriteKit

class Background {
    private let parallaxNode: ParallaxNode
    private let duration: Double

    init(textureNamed textureName: String, duration: Double) {
        parallaxNode = ParallaxNode(textureNamed: textureName)
        self.duration = duration
    }

    func addTo(parentNode: SKSpriteNode) -> Self {
        parallaxNode.addTo(parentNode)
        return self
    }
}
```

As you can see, the class saves the requested duration of a cycle, and then it forwards the calls to a class called `ParallaxNode`:

```
// Startable
extension Background : Startable {
    func start() {
        parallaxNode.start(duration: duration)
    }

    func stop() {
        parallaxNode.stop()
    }
}
```

The `Startable` protocol is implemented by forwarding the methods to `ParallaxNode`.

How to implement the scrolling

The idea of implementing scrolling is really straightforward: we implement a node where we put two copies of the same image in a tiled format. We then place the node such that we have the left half fully visible. Then we move the entire node to the left until we fully present the left node. Finally, we reset the position to the original one and restart the cycle.

The following figure explains this algorithm:

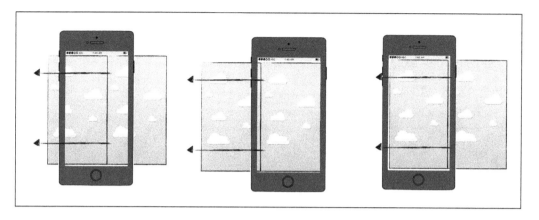

```
import SpriteKit

class ParallaxNode {
    private let node: SKSpriteNode!

    init(textureNamed: String) {
        let leftHalf = createHalfNodeTexture(textureNamed, offsetX: 0)
        let rightHalf = createHalfNodeTexture(textureNamed, offsetX:
leftHalf.size.width)

        let size = CGSize(width: leftHalf.size.width + rightHalf.size.
width,
            height: leftHalf.size.height)

        node = SKSpriteNode(color: UIColor.whiteColor(), size: size)
        node.anchorPoint = CGPointZero
        node.position = CGPointZero
        node.addChild(leftHalf)
        node.addChild(rightHalf)
    }

    func zPosition(zPosition: CGFloat) -> ParallaxNode {
        node.zPosition = zPosition
        return self
    }

    func addTo(parentNode: SKSpriteNode) -> ParallaxNode {
        parentNode.addChild(node)
        return self
    }
}
```

The init() method simply creates the two halves, puts them side by side, and sets the position of the node:

```
// Mark: Private
private func createHalfNodeTexture(textureNamed: String, offsetX:
CGFloat) -> SKSpriteNode {
   let node = SKSpriteNode(imageNamed: textureNamed,
                          normalMapped: true)
   node.anchorPoint = CGPointZero
   node.position = CGPoint(x: offsetX, y: 0)
   return node
}
```

The half node is just a node with the correct offset for the *x*-coordinate:

```
// Mark: Startable
extension ParallaxNode {
    func start(#duration: NSTimeInterval) {
        node.runAction(SKAction.repeatActionForever(SKAction.sequence(
            [
                SKAction.moveToX(-node.size.width/2.0, duration:
duration),
                SKAction.moveToX(0, duration: 0)
            ]
        )))
    }

    func stop() {
        node.removeAllActions()
    }
}
```

Finally, the Startable protocol is implemented using two actions in a sequence. First, we move half the size—which means an image width—to the left, and then we move the node to the original position to start the cycle again.

This is what the final result looks like:

 You can find the code for this version at `https://github.com/gscalzo/FlappySwift/tree/stage_with_parallax_levels`.

A flying bird

It's now the time to implement our hero.

Adding the Bird node

First of all, we must add a new character to `GameScene`:

```swift
class GameScene: SKScene {
    private var bird: Bird!
    //...
    override func didMoveToView(view: SKView) {
        //...
        bird = Bird(textureNames: ["bird1.png", "bird2.png"]).
addTo(screenNode)
        bird.position = CGPointMake(30.0, 400.0)

        actors = [sky, city, ground, bird]
        //...
    }
}
```

We can see that this new class behaves like the other, which we have already implemented:

```swift
import SpriteKit

class Bird : Startable {
    private var node: SKSpriteNode!
    private let textureNames: [String]

    var position : CGPoint {
        set { node.position = newValue }
        get { return node.position }
    }

    init(textureNames: [String]) {
        self.textureNames = textureNames
        node = createNode()
    }

    func addTo(scene: SKSpriteNode) -> Bird{
        scene.addChild(node)
        return self
    }
}
```

In the public part, we build the node and add it to the parent. Note that the position property is implemented as a computed property, which forwards set and get to the SKNode:

```
// Creators
private extension Bird {
    func createNode() -> SKSpriteNode {
        let birdNode = SKSpriteNode(imageNamed: textureNames.first!)
        birdNode.zPosition = 2.0
        return birdNode
    }
}
```

The node is built using the first frame of the passed textures. Also, the *z* position is set to be on top of all the background images:

```
// Startable
extension Bird : Startable {
    func start() {
        animate()
    }

    func stop() {
        node.physicsBody!.dynamic = false
        node.removeAllActions()
    }
}
// Private
extension Bird {
    private func animate(){
        let animationFrames = textureNames.map { texName in
            SKTexture(imageNamed: texName)
        }

        node.runAction(
            SKAction.repeatActionForever(
                SKAction.animateWithTextures(animationFrames,
timePerFrame: 0.5)
            ))
    }
}
```

The `start()` function animates the bird by alternating between the provided textures. The `stop()` function stops the animation and the physics. You'll understand better what this means in the next section:

```
// Actions
extension Bird {
    func update() {
        switch node.physicsBody!.velocity.dy {
        case let dy where dy > 30.0:
            node.zRotation = (3.14/6.0)
        case let dy where dy < -100.0:
            node.zRotation = -1*(3.14/4.0)
        default:
            node.zRotation = 0.0
        }
    }
}
```

Finally, the `update` method changes the rotation as per the vertical speed. Because the framework calls the `update` method of the current scene for every frame refresh, we need to forward it to the bird:

```
class GameScene: SKScene {
//...
    override func update(currentTime: CFTimeInterval) {
        bird.update()
    }
    //..
}
```

If we run the app now, we will see a cute bird flying, but it is stuck in the middle of the screen!

Making the bird flap

To implement the flight of the bird, we'll leverage the physics engine provided by SpriteKit. To use a physics engine, we must define a gravity force and then define the mass for each element we want to animate by following the laws of physics. It might sound complex, but in reality it's relatively straightforward.

First of all, we must define gravity in the scene:

```
class GameScene: SKScene {
    override func didMoveToView(view: SKView) {
        physicsWorld.gravity = CGVector(dx: 0, dy: -3)
```

```
    //..
    }
}
```

Next, we add the handling of touches:

```
class GameScene: SKScene {
//...
    override func touchesBegan(touches: Set<NSObject>, withEvent
event: UIEvent) {
        bird.flap()
    }
}
```

Pay attention: this is a *low-level* touching interception, and the proper "Apple" way is by using a gesture recognizer.

Then we add a physics body to the bird:

```
private extension Bird {
    func createNode() -> SKSpriteNode {
        let birdNode = SKSpriteNode(imageNamed: textureNames.first!)
        birdNode.zPosition = 2.0
        birdNode.physicsBody = SKPhysicsBody.rectSize(birdNode.size) {
            body in
            body.dynamic = true
            return
        }
        return birdNode
    }
}
```

The usual way to set up `SKPhysicsBody` is to create a body first and then mutate it by changing the values of its properties. As we prefer immutability, we extended `SKPhysicsBody` to handle the builder pattern, and this allows us to build and set `SKPhysics` in only one place and return an immutable object:

```
extension SKPhysicsBody {
    typealias BodyBuilderClosure = (SKPhysicsBody) -> ()

    class func rectSize(size: CGSize,
        builderClosure: BodyBuilderClosure) -> SKPhysicsBody {
            let body = SKPhysicsBody(rectangleOfSize: size)
            builderClosure(body)
            return body
    }
}
```

To simulate a flap, we apply an impulse to the bird in the direction opposite to gravity:

```
// Actions
extension Bird {
    func flap() {
        node.physicsBody!.velocity = CGVector(dx: 0, dy: 0)
        node.physicsBody!.applyImpulse(CGVector(dx: 0, dy: 8))
    }
    //...
}
```

By running the app now, we can make our bird fly:

 You can find the code for this version at https://github.com/gscalzo/FlappySwift/tree/the_bird.

Pipes!

Now the bird is flapping, but there are no enemies, so the game is pretty boring. It's time to add some obstacles—pipes!

Implementing the pipes node

To implement the pipes as they were in the original game, we need two classes: `PipesNode`, which contains the top and bottom pipes; and `Pipes`, which creates and handles `PipesNode`.

Let's begin with `Pipes` and add it as an actor to `GameScene`:

```
//...
let pipes = Pipes(topPipeTexture: "topPipe.png",
bottomPipeTexture: "bottomPipe").addTo(screenNode)

actors = [sky, city, ground, bird, pipes]
//...
```

The `Pipes` class holds the texture name, and it is added to the nodes tree:

```
import SpriteKit

class Pipes {
    private class var createActionKey : String { get {return
"createActionKey"} }
    private var parentNode: SKSpriteNode!
    private let topPipeTexture: String
    private let bottomPipeTexture: String

    init(topPipeTexture: String, bottomPipeTexture: String) {
        self.topPipeTexture = topPipeTexture
        self.bottomPipeTexture = bottomPipeTexture
    }

    func addTo(parentNode: SKSpriteNode) -> Pipes {
        self.parentNode = parentNode
        return self
    }
}
```

You can see here that the `Pipes` public interface is similar to that of the other nodes we have implemented so far:

```
//MARK: Startable
extension Pipes : Startable {
    func start() {
        let createAction = SKAction.repeatActionForever(
            SKAction.sequence(
                [
                    SKAction.runBlock {
                        self.createNewPipesNode()
                    },
                    SKAction.waitForDuration(3)
                ]
            ) )

        parentNode.runAction(createAction, withKey: Pipes.
createActionKey)
    }

    func stop() {
        parentNode.removeActionForKey(Pipes.createActionKey)

        let pipeNodes = parentNode.children.filter {
            ($0 as SKNode).name == PipesNode.kind
        }
        for pipe in pipeNodes {
            pipe.removeAllActions()
        }
    }
}
```

The `start` function basically creates a new `PipesNode` every three seconds, and the `stop` function removes the current action and the actions of the working `PipesNodes`:

```
//MARK: Private
private extension Pipes {
    func createNewPipesNode() {
        PipesNode(topPipeTexture: topPipeTexture, bottomPipeTexture:bo
ttomPipeTexture, centerY: centerPipes()).addTo(parentNode).start()
    }

    func centerPipes() -> CGFloat {
        return parentNode.size.height/2 - 100 + 20 *
CGFloat(arc4random_uniform(10))
    }
}
```

The `createNewPipesNode()` function creates a new `Pipes` pair. Add it to `parentNode` and start it. To create a pair of differently placed pipes every time, we use a function that calculates a random place for the center:

```
import SpriteKit

class PipesNode{
    class var kind : String { get {return "PIPES"} }
    private let gapSize: CGFloat = 50

    private let pipesNode: SKNode
    private let finalOffset: CGFloat!
    private let startingOffset: CGFloat!

    init(topPipeTexture: String, bottomPipeTexture: String, centerY:
CGFloat){
        pipesNode = SKNode()
        pipesNode.name = PipesNode.kind

        let pipeTop = createPipe(imageNamed: topPipeTexture)
        let pipeTopPosition = CGPoint(x: 0, y: centerY + pipeTop.size.
height/2 + gapSize)
        pipeTop.position = pipeTopPosition
        pipesNode.addChild(pipeTop)

        let pipeBottom = createPipe(imageNamed: bottomPipeTexture)
        let pipeBottomPosition = CGPoint(x: 0 , y: centerY -
pipeBottom.size.height/2 - gapSize)
        pipeBottom.position = pipeBottomPosition
        pipesNode.addChild(pipeBottom)

        finalOffset = -pipeBottom.size.width
        startingOffset = -finalOffset
    }
```

`PipesNode` is a node on top of which we place the two pipes' sprites. Note that in the constructor, we also calculate the starting and ending points of the pipes:

```
    func addTo(parentNode: SKSpriteNode) -> PipesNode {
        let pipePosition = CGPoint(x: parentNode.size.width +
startingOffset, y: 0)
        pipesNode.position = pipePosition
        pipesNode.zPosition = 4

        parentNode.addChild(pipesNode)
```

```
        return self
    }

    func start() {
        pipesNode.runAction(SKAction.sequence(
            [
                SKAction.moveToX(finalOffset, duration: 6.0),
                SKAction.removeFromParent()
            ]
        ))
    }
```

These values are used in `addTo()` to set the starting point, and in `start()`, where the first action commands the node to move towards the left, outside the screen, before removing the node from the parent:

```
// Creators
func createPipe(#imageNamed: String) -> SKSpriteNode {
    let pipeNode = SKSpriteNode(imageNamed: imageNamed)
    return pipeNode
}
```

With the implementation of this constructor function, we are ready to run the app and see how it looks.

And it looks really pretty! But the pipes are in front of the ground, not behind it as expected. This issue can be solved easily by changing the `zPosition` of the ground, making it greater than that of the pipes.

You have probably noticed that we have set the `zPosition` of the pipes at a well-defined value, but it's still not compiling:

```
        func addTo(parentNode: SKSpriteNode) -> PipesNode {
            //...
    pipesNode.zPosition = 4
            //...
    }
```

First, we need to expose `zPosition` in the `Background` class, and we do this by adding a forwarding function:

```
    class Background {
    //...
        func zPosition(zPosition: CGFloat) {
            parallaxNode.zPosition(zPosition)
        }
    //...
    }
```

Then we change it during the process of building the actors:

```
        let ground = Background(textureNamed: "ground", duration:5.0).
    addTo(screenNode)
        ground.zPosition(5)
```

Run the app now; everything works as expected, as shown in this screenshot:

 You can find the code for this version at `https://github.com/` `gscalzo/FlappySwift/tree/pipes`.

Making the components interact

Although the app is colorful and seeing the bird fly is fun, we need to create a scene like the real world, where collision with an obstacle typically brings you to a halt.

Setting up the collision detection engine

The SpriteKit physics engine provides us with a really simple mechanism to detect collisions between objects. Basically, we need to set a bitmask for each component, and then a collision detection delegate. Let start defining the bitmask; for it, we define an enumeration in GameScene:

```
enum BodyType : UInt32 {
    case bird   = 1  // 0b0001
    case ground = 2  // 0b0010
    case pipe   = 4  // 0b0100
    case gap    = 8  // 0b1000
}
```

Pay attention to two things: the first is that we must define the bitmask as a power of 2; so that we can detect what touches what, using a bitwise or operation. The second is that we've added a gap identifier, a component we haven't defined yet.

The gap is the hole between two pipes, and we need to detect the moment when the bird passes through this hole to increase the score.

Let's start setting up the pipes:

```
func createPipe(#imageNamed: String) -> SKSpriteNode {
    let pipeNode = SKSpriteNode(imageNamed: imageNamed)
    let size = CGSize(width: pipeNode.size.width,
                      height: pipeNode.size.height)
    pipeNode.physicsBody = SKPhysicsBody.rectSize(size) {
        body in
        body.dynamic             = false
        body.affectedByGravity   = false
        body.categoryBitMask     = BodyType.pipe.rawValue
        body.collisionBitMask    = BodyType.pipe.rawValue
    }

    return pipeNode
}
```

Basically, we have defined the physics for the pipes:

Also we took advantage of being already here to add the gap component:

```
private func createGap(#size: CGSize) -> SKSpriteNode {
    let gapNode = SKSpriteNode(color: UIColor.clearColor(),
        size: size)
    gapNode.zPosition = 6
    gapNode.physicsBody = SKPhysicsBody.rectSize(size) {
        body in
        body.dynamic = false
        body.affectedByGravity = false
        body.categoryBitMask = BodyType.gap.rawValue
        body.collisionBitMask = BodyType.gap.rawValue
    }
    return gapNode
}
```

The definition is pretty similar to that of the Pipe:

```
init(topPipeTexture: String, bottomPipeTexture: String, centerY:
CGFloat){
//...
    pipesNode.addChild(pipeBottom)

    let gapNode = createGap(size: CGSize(
        width: pipeBottom.size.width,
        height: gapSize*2))
    gapNode.position = CGPoint(x: 0, y: centerY)
    pipesNode.addChild(gapNode)
    //...
}
```

The gap is simply set as a node and put in the node tree. Let's move on to the bird now:

```
// Creators
private extension Bird {
    func createNode() -> SKSpriteNode {
        let birdNode = SKSpriteNode(imageNamed: textureNames.first!)
        birdNode.zPosition = 2.0
        birdNode.physicsBody = SKPhysicsBody.rectSize(birdNode.size.
scale(0.8)){
            body in
            body.dynamic = true
            body.categoryBitMask = BodyType.bird.rawValue
            body.collisionBitMask = BodyType.bird.rawValue
```

```
            body.contactTestBitMask = BodyType.ground.rawValue |
                BodyType.pipe.rawValue |
                BodyType.gap.rawValue
        }

        return birdNode
    }
}
```

We are concentrating the detection logic inside the bird class, saying that the bird touches the ground, the pipe, or the gap.

Note that we are reducing the actual size of the related body of the bird. This is because the bird's frames have a transparent border in order to contain the wing animation, and using the entire frame would have made the detection area larger than needed.

Pay attention to this code; `scale()` is an extension we add to `CGSize`:

```
// CGSize Private
extension CGSize {
    func scale(factor: CGFloat) -> CGSize {
        return CGSize(width: self.width * factor, height: self.height
* factor)
    }
}
```

We set the delegate in `GameScene`:

```
override func didMoveToView(view: SKView) {
    physicsWorld.contactDelegate = self
    //...
}
```

After setting it, we implement the protocol:

```
// Contacts
extension GameScene: SKPhysicsContactDelegate {
    func didBeginContact(contact: SKPhysicsContact) {
        let contactMask = contact.bodyA.categoryBitMask | contact.
bodyB.categoryBitMask

        switch (contactMask) {
        case BodyType.pipe.rawValue | BodyType.bird.rawValue:
            println("Contact with a pipe")
        case BodyType.ground.rawValue | BodyType.bird.rawValue:
            println("Contact with ground")
```

```
        for actor in actors {
            actor.stop()
        }
    default:
        return
    }


}

func didEndContact(contact: SKPhysicsContact) {
    let contactMask = contact.bodyA.categoryBitMask | contact.
bodyB.categoryBitMask

    switch (contactMask) {
    case BodyType.gap.rawValue | BodyType.bird.rawValue:
        println("Contact with gap")
    default:
        return
    }
}
}
```

You can see from the code, that using the bitmask helps us know which two objects are colliding, without requiring the knowledge of which object is in bodyA and which is in bodyB.

By running the app now, you can see that everything works fine when the bird collides with either the pipes or the gap, but nothing happens in the case of the ground. This is because the ground is currently a SKSpriteNode, and it has no body associated with it.

Let's solve this issue by adding a function to GameScene. This function creates a body for the ground:

```
override func didMoveToView(view: SKView) {
//...
    ground.zPosition(5)
    screenNode.addChild(bodyTextureName("ground"))
    //...
}
```

The function for creating the body is really straightforward:

```
private extension GameScene{
    func bodyTextureName(textureName: String) -> SKNode{
        let image = UIImage(named: textureName)
        let width = image!.size.width
        let height = image!.size.height
        let groundBody = SKNode()
        groundBody.position = CGPoint(x: width/2, y: height/2)

        groundBody.physicsBody = SKPhysicsBody.rectSize(CGSize(width:
width, height: height)){ body in
            body.dynamic = false
            body.affectedByGravity = false
            body.categoryBitMask = BodyType.ground.rawValue
            body.collisionBitMask = BodyType.ground.rawValue
        }

        return groundBody
    }
}
```

Before trying the app, we set up the debug settings to show the shape of every physics body in the game:

```
class GameViewController: UIViewController {
override func viewDidLoad() {
//...
        if let scene = GameScene.unarchiveFromFile("GameScene") as?
GameScene {
//...
            skView.showsPhysics = true
            //...
}
    }
}
```

By running the app now, we can see from the log that we are interacting with all the required components, as shown in the following screenshot:

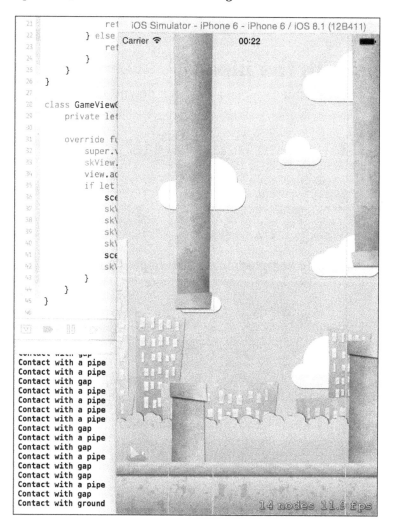

 You can find the code for this version at https://github.com/ gscalzo/FlappySwift/tree/collision_detection.

Completing the game

Almost everything is done now, and in this final section, we are going to add the correct interaction between all the elements of the game.

Colliding with the pipes

When the bird touches a pipe, we need to push it down so that it touches the ground and dies:

```
extension GameScene: SKPhysicsContactDelegate {
    func didBeginContact(contact: SKPhysicsContact!) {
//...
        case BodyType.pipe.rawValue | BodyType.bird.rawValue:
            println("Contact with a pipe")
            bird.pushDown()
            //...
    }
}
```

To push it, we can use the same technique that we used for the flapping – apply an impulse:

```
func pushDown() {
    dying = true
    node.physicsBody!.applyImpulse(CGVector(dx: 0, dy: -10))
}
```

Although the impulse has been applied correctly, you might notice that you can continue flapping after touching a pipe, and sometimes the bird starts flying again.

To solve this issue, we add a status variable to the bird. This variable indicates whether the bird is dying or alive:

```
class Bird : Startable {
    //...
private var dying = false
    //...
}
extension Bird {
    func flap() {
        if !dying {
            node.physicsBody!.velocity = CGVector(dx: 0, dy: 0)
            node.physicsBody!.applyImpulse(CGVector(dx: 0, dy: 6))
        }
    }
    //...
}
```

Now the bird has no way to save itself after hitting a pipe!

Adding the score

The last feature that is missing is the score.

First of all, we implement a Score class. It holds the current score and the label used to present it:

```
import SpriteKit

class Score {
    private let score = SKLabelNode(text: "0")
    var currentScore = 0

func addTo(parentNode: SKSpriteNode) -> Score {
        score.fontName = "MarkerFelt-Wide"
        score.fontSize = 30
        score.position = CGPoint(x: parentNode.size.width/2, y:
parentNode.size.height - 40)
        parentNode.addChild(score)
        return self
    }

    func increase() {
        currentScore += 1
        score.text = "\(currentScore)"
    }
}
```

We then need to add it to the main screen:

```
class GameScene: SKScene {
//...
    private var score = Score()

    override func didMoveToView(view: SKView) {
//...
score.addTo(screenNode)
//...
    }
}
```

Next, we increase the score after the bird leaves a gap:

```
    func didEndContact(contact: SKPhysicsContact!) {
        //...
    switch (contactMask) {
```

```
case BodyType.gap.rawValue | BodyType.bird.rawValue:
    println("Contact with gap")
    score.increase()
    //...
    }
}
```

Then we can play and see our score increase.

Adding a restarting popup

You must have surely noticed that after the bird dies, the only way to play again is by restarting the app. Pretty annoying, isn't it?

Let's add a popup to present the final score and allow the player to play again. To get a nicer alert view, we use the SIAlertView pod by adding the pod 'SIAlertView' line to our Podfile.

Then we add a handler to manage the end of the game:

```
case BodyType.ground.rawValue | BodyType.bird.rawValue:
    println("Contact with ground")
    for actor in actors {
        actor.stop()
    }
    askToPlayAgain()
```

The askToPlayAgain() function basically builds the popup:

```
// Private
private extension GameScene {
    func askToPlayAgain() {
        let alertView = SIAlertView(title: "Ouch!!", andMessage:
"Congratulations! Your score is \(score.currentScore). Play again?")

        alertView.addButtonWithTitle("OK", type: .Default) { _ in
self.onPlayAgainPressed() }
        alertView.addButtonWithTitle("Cancel", type: .Default) { _ in
self.onCancelPressed() }
        alertView.show()
    }
}
```

Don't forget to import the correct framework and add two public properties to hold the callbacks associated with the two buttons:

```
import SpriteKit
import SIAlertView

class GameScene: SKScene {
//...
var onPlayAgainPressed:(()->Void)!
    var onCancelPressed:(()->Void)!
```

Next, we need to refactor the `GameViewController` class to extract the creation of the scene in an independent function to permit calling inside the callback:

```
class GameViewController: UIViewController {
    private let skView = SKView()

    override func viewDidLoad() {
        super.viewDidLoad()
        skView.frame = view.bounds
        view.addSubview(skView)
        createTheScene()
    }
    private func createTheScene() {
        if let scene = GameScene.unarchiveFromFile("GameScene") as?
GameScene {
            scene.size = skView.frame.size
            skView.showsPhysics = true
            skView.showsFPS = true
            skView.showsNodeCount = true
            skView.ignoresSiblingOrder = true
            scene.scaleMode = .AspectFill

            scene.onPlayAgainPressed = {[weak self] in
                self?.createTheScene()
                return
            }
            scene.onCancelPressed = {[weak self] in
                self?.dismissViewControllerAnimated(true, completion:
nil)
                return
            }
            self.skView.presentScene(scene)
        }
    }
}
```

Finally, the game has all the required features, and they make it fun.

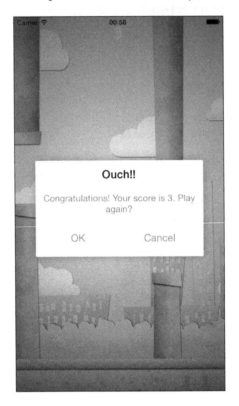

  You can find the code for this version at `https://github.com/gscalzo/FlappySwift/tree/full_plain_game`.

Summary

In this chapter, we shifted gears and introduced a new framework. You learned about the most common and useful features when it comes to building a video game.

You also learned how to implement scrolling using different speeds to simulate depth. Then we added a character, animated it, and made it move.

Finally, we introduced a physics engine. It is useful for many purposes, including collision detection.

Although the game is functionally complete, in the next chapter, we'll continue to polish it by adding music, video, sound effects, and a connection to the Game Center.

6

Polishing Flappy Swift

We ended the previous chapter with a complete clone of *Flappy Bird*.

Although the game is fun and you can play exactly as you do in the original, you might have noticed that the game is lacking something that makes professional games more interesting to play.

The goal of this chapter is to fill this lacuna by adding some *juiciness* and integrating the game with the Game Center to create a leaderboard and increase engagement of your players.

Adding juiciness

Juiciness in a game or an app can be defined as all the effects such as sounds, zooming, or shaking elements. Although they are not indispensable to the game, they make the experience of gaming more pleasant.

Let there be sounds!

The first thing we add is the sound effects, to give feedback to the user when something, either good or bad, happens in the game. For example, we could notify that the bird is flapping, or has hit the pipes, using a sound.

There are basically two ways for an indie game developer — which means a developer without any video game publisher's financial support — to add sounds to the game: creating them, or searching for them from sound collections such as `https://www.freesound.org` or `http://www.freesfx.co.uk`.

Because the aim of this book is to teach you how to create apps using Swift, we'll use some resources found in a free collection.

In the master branch, you can find .zip files with all the required sounds.

[ You can find the sounds at https://github.com/gscalzo/
FlappySwift/blob/master/sounds.zip?raw=true.]

Let's start adding them to the project by creating a new folder in it, like this:

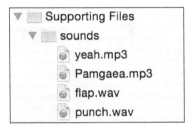

SpriteKit provides us with a convenient action to play a sound, and we don't have to worry about the format of the sound.

However, you must pay attention to the fact that uncompressed files, such as .wav, can have a large size, and the resulting app can become larger than expected. So, I advise you to always convert sound files into .mp3 files.

That said, let's add the sound of flapping to be played when the player touches the screen. Add this code to the GameScene file:

```
override func touchesBegan(touches: NSSet, withEvent event:
UIEvent) {
    runAction(SKAction.playSoundFileNamed("flap.wav",
waitForCompletion: false))
    bird.flap()
}
```

By starting the app now, we can hear a sound effect when the bird flaps its wings.

As you can imagine, adding a "bump" sound when the bird hits a pipe or the ground is just matter of writing a similar function call in the correct place:

```
func didBeginContact(contact: SKPhysicsContact!) {
    //...
    switch (contactMask) {
    case BodyType.pipe.rawValue | BodyType.bird.rawValue:
        println("Contact with a pipe")
        runAction(SKAction.playSoundFileNamed("punch.wav",
waitForCompletion: false))
```

```
        bird.pushDown()
    case BodyType.ground.rawValue | BodyType.bird.rawValue:
        println("Contact with ground")
        runAction(SKAction.playSoundFileNamed("punch.wav",
waitForCompletion: false))
        for actor in actors {
            actor.stop()
        }
    //...
    }
}
```

Finally, we add a cheerful sound when the player gets a point:

```
func didEndContact(contact: SKPhysicsContact!) {
    //...
    switch (contactMask) {
    case BodyType.gap.rawValue |  BodyType.bird.rawValue:
        println("Contact with gap")
        runAction(SKAction.playSoundFileNamed("yeah.mp3",
waitForCompletion: false))
        score.increase()
        //...
    }
}
```

When you play the app, you will notice that it's already very pleasant to play.

Playing the soundtrack

Kevin MacLeod's site, http://incompetech.com, is a virtually infinite source of amazing free video game and movie soundtracks. There, you can find tons of amazing .mp3 files under the Creative Commons Attribution License. We are going to use one of Kevin's files, *Pamgaea*, which can be found at http://incompetech.com/wordpress/2013/09/pamgaea/.

Although we can use the SpriteKit action to play the soundtrack, it is better to use AVFoundation. It can give us more flexibility in playing a long sound file.

Let's start implementing a proper class to handle the player:

```
import Foundation
import AVFoundation

class MusicPlayer {
    private let player: AVAudioPlayer?
```

```
    init?(filename: String, type: String){
        if let resource = NSBundle.mainBundle().
pathForResource(filename, ofType: type) {
            let url = NSURL(fileURLWithPath: resource)
            player = AVAudioPlayer(contentsOfURL: url, error: nil);
            player!.numberOfLoops = -1
            player!.prepareToPlay()
        } else {
            player = nil
            return nil
        }
    }
}
```

This class basically wraps AVPlayer to configure it to play infinite loops (this is the meaning of the player!.numberOfLoops = -1 statement). It also preloads part of the song in its internal cache before it receives the play() call.

As you can see, the initializer is marked as init?. This means that it can return a nil value, if the resources needed for building it are missing—the sound file in our case.

The only two functions we need are play() and stop(), which are basically a forward to the actual AVPlayer:

```
class MusicPlayer {
    //...
    func play() {
        if let player = player {
            player.play()
        }
    }
    func stop() {
        if let player = player {
            player.stop()
        }
    }
}
```

We want to start playing when the app starts, so we add the player to MenuViewController:

```
class MenuViewController: UIViewController {
    //...
    private let player = MusicPlayer(filename: "Pamgaea", type: "mp3")
```

```
        override func viewDidLoad() {
            super.viewDidLoad()
            player?.play()
     //...
         }
   }
```

Start the app. A funny tune will follow, playing during the gameplay.

Shaking the screen!

If you have ever played the original game, you might remember that the screen shook whenever the bird hit the ground. Although an action to make a node shake doesn't exist, we can add a new action, which is basically a sequence of moving around the center:

```
extension SKAction {
    // Thanks to Benzi: http://stackoverflow.com/a/24769521/288379
class func shake(duration:CGFloat, amplitudeX:Int = 3, amplitudeY:Int
= 3) -> SKAction {
        let numberOfShakes = duration / 0.015 / 2.0
        var actionsArray:[SKAction] = []
        for index in 1...Int(numberOfShakes) {
            let dx = CGFloat(arc4random_uniform(UInt32(amplitudeX))) -
CGFloat(amplitudeX / 2)
            let dy = CGFloat(arc4random_uniform(UInt32(amplitudeY))) -
CGFloat(amplitudeY / 2)
            let forward = SKAction.moveByX(dx, y:dy, duration: 0.015)
            let reverse = forward.reversedAction()
            actionsArray.append(forward)
            actionsArray.append(reverse)
        }
        return SKAction.sequence(actionsArray)
    }
}
```

We use this action when the bird hits the ground. It is applied to the screen node:

```
extension GameScene: SKPhysicsContactDelegate {
    func didBeginContact(contact: SKPhysicsContact!) {
        //...
        case BodyType.ground.rawValue | BodyType.bird.rawValue:
        //...
            let shakeAction = SKAction.shake(0.1, amplitudeX: 20,
amplitudeY: 20)
            screenNode.runAction(shakeAction)
            self.askToPlayAgain()
        //...
}
```

By playing the app, you will notice that the screen shakes, but the effect is reduced by the appearance of the popup asking for a restart. The faster way to fix this issue is to add a small delay before the popup appears.

Because the function for executing a delayed block could be handy for other apps, we wrap the actual GDC function in a function:

```
import Foundation
func execAfter(delay:Double, closure:()->()) {
    dispatch_after(
        dispatch_time(
            DISPATCH_TIME_NOW,
            Int64(delay * Double(NSEC_PER_SEC))
        ),
        dispatch_get_main_queue(), closure)
}
```

So, we can delay the popup in this way:

```
let shakeAction = SKAction.shake(0.1, amplitudeX: 20,
                                      amplitudeY: 20)
screenNode.runAction(shakeAction)
execAfter(1) {
    self.askToPlayAgain()
}
```

The app is now complete from the features point of view, and we can move on to add Game Center support.

 You can find the code for this version at `https://github.com/gscalzo/FlappySwift/tree/juicy`.

Integrating with Game Center

Game Center can be defined as a social gaming network that offers multiplayer features. It was made available in iOS 4.1, and it has been updated with new gaming options ever since.

What Game Center provides

The features provided by Game Center are as follows:

- **Leaderboards**: This is a shared database containing the scores of the players of the game. It allows them to add their personal results and compare them with the scores of other players.

- **Achievements**: These are the goals defined inside the game that cause players to maintain interest in the game. Some examples of achievements can be **Destroyed 50 enemies**, **Run during the night**, and so on.

- **Multiplayer**: This feature allows the developer to implement a networked game where players can compete with each other, either in real time or in a turn-based manner.

Incorporating Game Center into an app is a two-step project. First of all, we need to set up the app in iTunes Connect, enabling Game Center support and setting up the leaderboards. Then we need to add the code to send the score to Game Center.

Setting up Game Center

We'll use Xcode to automate the tasks to be done, to set up Game Center:

1. The first thing we need to do, is to add an Apple ID to Xcode. Go to **Xcode menu | Preferences** and select the **Accounts** icon, as shown in this screenshot:

2. Then we add the Apple ID, as shown in the following screenshot:

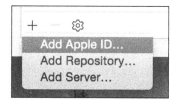

3. Now, in the project navigator, select the project and the correct name of the team, which should be the name of the developer, like this:

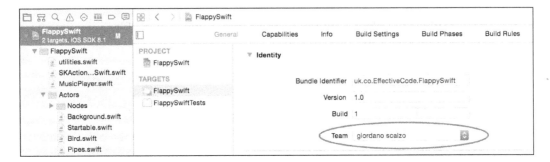

4. Finally, click on **Capabilities** at the top of the window and turn on the switch for Game Center, as shown in this screenshot:

Before implementing the code, we need to set up the App on iTunes Connect.

Creating an app record on iTunes Connect

Creating a record in iTunes Connect is not mandatory for integrating with Game Center, but it is necessary for creating any leaderboard. If you feel comfortable with this process, you can skip this section and go to the next section.

First of all, log in to iTunes Connect (`http://itunesconnect.apple.com`) using your credentials. Then add a new app by selecting the following icon:

By pressing the **+** sign at the top, we can add the app, as shown in this screenshot:

To complete the creation of the app, we fill in all of the required data, as shown in the following screenshot:

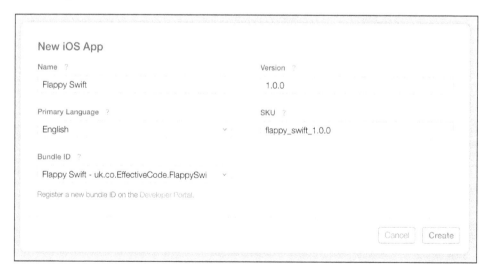

As you can see, the app ID we have created in Xcode is presented in the **Bundle ID** drop-down window so that we can add it as a bundle ID.

Here is a screenshot that shows the expected properties of the app:

Enabling Game Center

We have already enabled Game Center for the app in Xcode. We need to do the same for the app in iTunes Connect.

To do this, we must select **Game Center** from the menu of the app, as shown in the preceding screenshot.

Because we don't have a suite of games for sharing leaderboards, we select **Single Game**, like this:

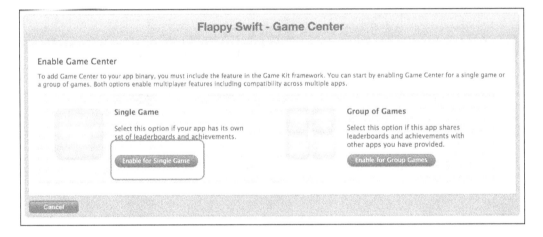

The following screenshot shows the enabled Game Center dashboard in our app:

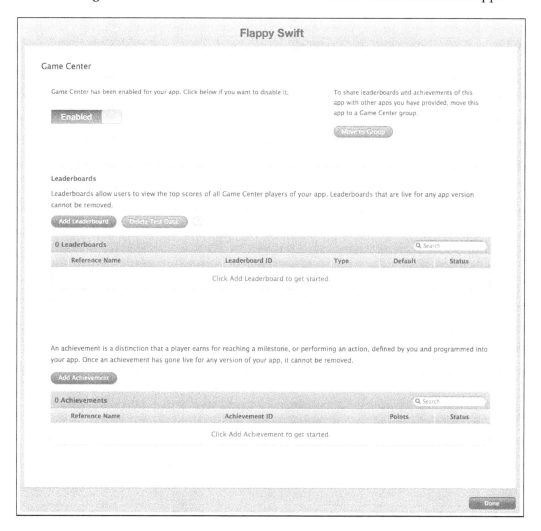

As you can see, we have the ability to add, change and configure several leaderboards and achievements, but for the sake of simplicity, we will create only one leaderboard. We do this by clicking on the **Add Leaderboard** button and filling in the form, as shown in this screenshot:

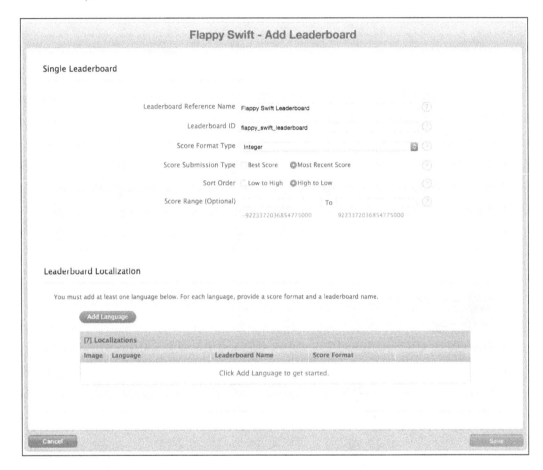

Finally, we have set up the leaderboard for our game.

Creating fake user accounts to test Game Center

Although not mandatory, it is definitely good practice to have fake test accounts for use during the development of a game that supports Game Center. Otherwise, you might risk having a not-yet-published app featured in Game Center.

To create new users, go back to the home page of iTunes Connect and then select the **Users and Roles** icon, which looks like this:

Then select **Sandbox Testers**, as shown in the following screenshot:

Finally, create the tester by filling in the form, like this:

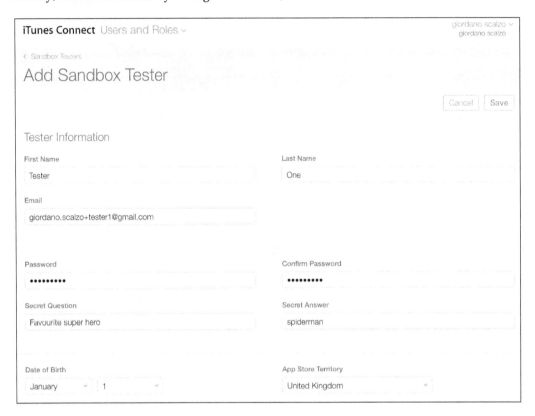

Although this process could seem awkward and long, after you learn to do it for an app, you'll notice that it will be always the same for all other apps you'll create supporting Game Center.

We are finally ready to add the code to enable the sharing of the code on Game Center.

Authenticating a player

The first thing that we must handle with the integration of Game Center, is to authenticate the player. Once the player is connected to Game Center, then all the features implemented in the app are available for them, otherwise they are simply not available.

Apple recommends implementing the authentication in `AppDelegate`, but we prefer to implement it as the first action in `MenuViewController`. To do this, we create a `GameCenter` wrapper class and use it in the `viewDidLoad()` function of `MenuViewController`:

```
class MenuViewController: UIViewController {
    //...
    private let gameCenter = GameCenter()
    override func viewDidLoad() {
        super.viewDidLoad()
        gameCenter.authenticateLocalPlayer()
    //...
```

Let's start implementing the `GameCenter` class:

```
import GameKit
import SIAlertView

class GameCenter: NSObject {
    private var gameCenterEnabled = false
    private var leaderboardIdentifier = ""

    func authenticateLocalPlayer() {
        let localPlayer = GKLocalPlayer.localPlayer()
        localPlayer.authenticateHandler = {
(viewController, error) in
            if let vc = viewController {
                let topViewController = UIApplication.
sharedApplication().delegate!.window!!.rootViewController
                topViewController?.presentViewController(vc, animated:
true, completion: nil)
            } else if localPlayer.authenticated {
                self?.gameCenterEnabled = true
                localPlayer.
loadDefaultLeaderboardIdentifierWithCompletionHandler(
                    { (leaderboardIdentifier, error) -> Void in
                        self?.leaderboardIdentifier =
leaderboardIdentifier
                        return
                })
            }
        }
    }
```

This class has two properties: a Boolean indicating whether Game Center is enabled or not, and the identifier for the leaderboard. Although we have set the name of the leaderboard and it is a constant, it's safer to retrieve it from the server to give us the flexibility to change it after the app has been published.

The code is really straightforward because it relies on the API of Game Center. Everything is handled by the `authenticateHandler()` closure, which is called by passing two optional values: a `UIViewController` and an error.

The former is the login ViewController that we must present when the user is not logged in. To find the topmost ViewController, we ask the `rootViewController` of the main window. If the user is connected, we retrieve the identifier of the leaderboard.

When the app is run, either the login screen or a banner with the name of the logged-in player should be presented, like this:

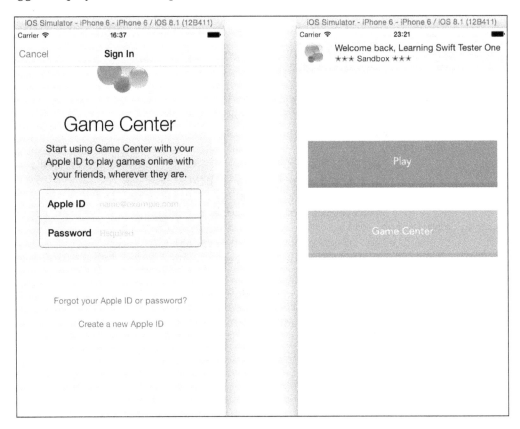

The rest of the class is just a function meant to report the scores, which basically transforms the score into an integer for the proper class:

```
class GameCenter: NSObject {
    //...
    func reportScore(score: Int){
        if !gameCenterEnabled {
            return
        }
        let gkScore = GKScore(leaderboardIdentifier:
leaderboardIdentifier)
        gkScore.value = Int64(score)
GKScore.reportScores([gkScore], withCompletionHandler: nil)
    }
}
```

The last of the required functions is a way of presenting the leaderboard:

```
class GameCenter: NSObject {
    //...
func showLeaderboard() {
        if !gameCenterEnabled {
            let alertView = SIAlertView(title: "Game Center
Unavailable", andMessage: "Player is not signed in")

            alertView.addButtonWithTitle("OK", type: .Default) { _ in
}
            alertView.show()
            return
        }
  let gcViewController = GKGameCenterViewController()

        gcViewController.gameCenterDelegate = self
        gcViewController.viewState = .Leaderboards
        gcViewController.leaderboardIdentifier = leaderboardIdentifier

        let topViewController = UIApplication.sharedApplication().
delegate!.window!!.rootViewController
        topViewController?.presentViewController(gcViewController,
animated: true, completion: nil)
    }
}
```

The `GKGameCenterControllerDelegate` protocol implementation simply dismisses the leaderboard ViewController:

```
extension GameCenter: GKGameCenterControllerDelegate {
    func gameCenterViewControllerDidFinish(gameCenterViewController:
GKGameCenterViewController) {
        gameCenterViewController.dismissViewControllerAnimated(true,
completion: nil)
    }
}
```

After implementing these functions, we need to add them to `MenuViewController`:

```
@objc func onPlayPressed(sender: UIButton) {
    let vc = GameViewController()
    vc.gameCenter = gameCenter
    //...
}

@objc func onGameCenterPressed(sender: UIButton) {
    gameCenter.showLeaderboard()
}
```

The `GameViewController` forwards the class to `GameScene`:

```
class GameViewController: UIViewController {
    var gameCenter: GameCenter?
    //...
private func createTheScene() {
        if let scene = GameScene.unarchiveFromFile("GameScene") as?
GameScene {
            scene.gameCenter = gameCenter
```

In the `GameScene` class, we report the score when the bird hits the ground:

```
class GameScene: SKScene {
  var gameCenter: GameCenter?
    //...
}
extension GameScene: SKPhysicsContactDelegate {
    func didBeginContact(contact: SKPhysicsContact!) {
        //...
        case BodyType.ground.rawValue | BodyType.bird.rawValue:
        //...
            if let gameCenter = gameCenter {
                gameCenter.reportScore(score.currentScore)
            }
```

With this code in place, after pressing the proper button, we can finally see the leaderboard, as shown in this screenshot:

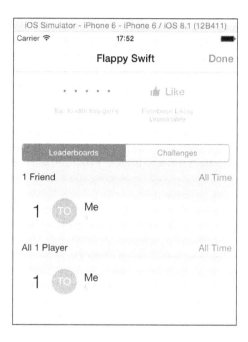

 You can find the code for this version at `https://github.com/gscalzo/FlappySwift/tree/gamecenter`.

Summary

This chapter was a bit different from the others because, for the first time, we probably spent more time configuring iTunes Connect than doing actual coding. However, this is a necessary step in order to include Game Center support, so it's worth gaining solid knowledge of how to do it.

With this chapter done—by adding juiciness and Game Center support—our "Flappy Swift" is ready to be published. So, it's time to move on to the next chapter, where we'll explore the other game development frameworks brought by iOS 8, by implementing a clone of an endless three-dimensional runner game called *Cube Runner*.

7
Cube Runner

In the last two chapters, we saw how easy it is to implement a 2D game using SpriteKit.

Probably, most of you think that implementing a 3D game is something that only professional game developers can do, because it needs knowledge of 3D graphics, math, rendering, lights, and so on, as well as external tools such as Unity.

That might have been true until Apple released SceneKit, a really simple 3D rendering framework, created mainly for hobbyists and casual game developers. First introduced in OS X Mountain Lion, it became even more powerful in 2014, with the addition of particle effects, physics simulation, and multipass rendering. It was added to iOS 8, allowing the community of iOS developers to implement 3D applications using a model similar to Sprite Kit and UIKit in general.

In this chapter, after a brief introduction to SceneKit using Playground, we'll implement an iOS clone of a fun Flash game.

The app is…

The world of Flash games is a never-ending source of inspiration, and because Flash is not available in iOS, the most fun Flash games must be remade in a native way.

Cube Runner is a rare case a in which simplicity and fun come together to create a really addictive game. Implemented in 2006 by Max Abernethy, it is a predecessor of the infinite runner game where the player, who is driving a triangular spaceship, must survive in an alien landscape by avoiding the cubes he encounters during the run.

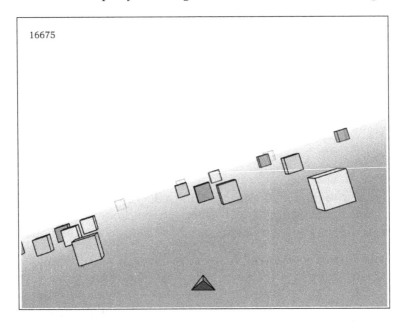

As is usual in endless runner games, the score increments in a time-based fashion; the more time the player survives, the bigger the score.

Introduction to SceneKit

Before diving into the development of the game, let's introduce SceneKit briefly.

What is SceneKit?

SceneKit is a rendering engine based on a hierarchy of nodes, similar to Sprite Kit. The most important kinds of nodes are lights, the camera, geometry objects, boxes, spheres, and so on. Actually, all of these are attributes of a node, but for the sake of simplicity of the mental model, let's consider these as different entities.

To these nodes, we can apply several actions, such as moving, rotating, and so on. We can also add a physical body to a node and put it into a physical world, which is again really similar to SpriteKit.

Building an empty scene

To get our feet wet, we'll use the playground again, as in the first chapter.

Let's start creating a new iOS playground called `SceneKitPlayground` and import the frameworks needed to perform our experiment:

```
import UIKit
import SceneKit
import XCPlayground
```

The latter is the framework that permits the display of the scene on the Playground console, so don't forget to open the console by going to **View | Assistant Editor | Show Assistant Editor**.

We start by creating an `SCNView`, which is the `UIView` that displays the SceneKit's scene. Then we add the scene, which is the stage where everything happens, and finally we show the view in the console:

```
var sceneView = SCNView(frame:
    CGRect(x: 0, y: 0,
        width: 400, height: 400))
var scene = SCNScene()
sceneView.scene = scene

XCPShowView("SceneView", sceneView)
```

This is what the playground presents:

```
|  <    >  |  ⬛ SceneKitPlayground.playground  > No Selection
1  import UIKit
2  import SceneKit
3  import XCPlayground
4
5  var sceneView = SCNView(frame:                          SCNView
6      CGRect(x: 0, y: 0,
7          width: 400, height: 400))
8  var scene = SCNScene()                                  SCNScene
9  sceneView.scene = scene                                 SCNView
10
11 XCPShowView("SceneView", sceneView)
```

Pay attention to the fact that we need to enable the playground to run inside the simulator, otherwise the scene will not be rendered and the console will be empty.

To enable it, we need to show the utility view. Go to **View** | **Utilities** | **Show Utilities**, and then select **Run in Full Simulator** in **Playground Settings**, as shown in this screenshot:

Now let's start adding the nodes to the scene, starting with the camera:

```
var camera = SCNCamera()
var cameraNode = SCNNode()
cameraNode.camera = camera
cameraNode.position = SCNVector3(x: 0, y: 0, z: 4)
scene.rootNode.addChildNode(cameraNode)
```

As mentioned earlier, the camera is an attribute of a node that can be positioned and rotated in the space of the scene. As you can see, an SCNScene has a predefined rootNode to which we add the children to create the object hierarchy.

Let's utilize this snippet of code to introduce the coordinate system of SceneKit, as follows:

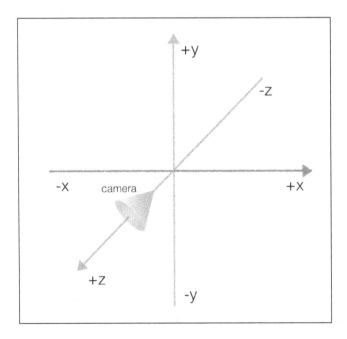

As you can see, the x and y axes are placed on the plane in front of the user, with the y axis being positive from bottom to top, the opposite of UIKit. The z axis runs from the user to the screen, with positive values towards the user. It's really important to be clear in your mind how these axes are orientated. Otherwise, it may become really difficult to place objects in the scene and debug them if the scene is not rendered as expected.

Adding a green torus

Now let's add an object to the scene:

```
var torus = SCNTorus(ringRadius: 1, pipeRadius: 0.35)
var torusNode = SCNNode(geometry: torus)
torusNode.position = SCNVector3(x: 0.0, y: 0.0, z: 0.0)
scene.rootNode.addChildNode(torusNode)
```

Despite us having added a camera and an object, nothing is shown in the scene.

This is because we haven't defined the material of the object yet. By material, we mean a collection of attributes associated with a surface that define its appearance when rendered. Using its properties, we can define it as opaque or transparent, how much light it can reflect or diffuse, and so on.

Let's define the torus as a green object that reflects white light:

```
torus.firstMaterial?.diffuse.contents  = UIColor.greenColor()
torus.firstMaterial?.specular.contents = UIColor.whiteColor()
```

Finally, a torus is rendered into the scene.

However, it's not really appealing. Because of the position of the camera, what we are seeing is basically the side of the torus. Also, instead of looking 3D, it appears really flat, like this:

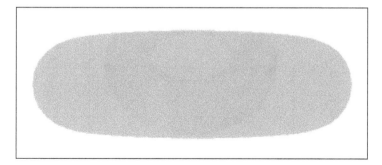

Let's solve the first issue by rotating the torus by π/4 around the *x* axis:

```
torusNode.rotation = SCNVector4(x: 1.0, y: 0.0, z: 0.0, w: Float(M_
PI/4.0))
```

To rotate a node, we first need to define the vector around which the node will rotate, and then the angle of the rotation. Now the torus is nicely visible, as shown here:

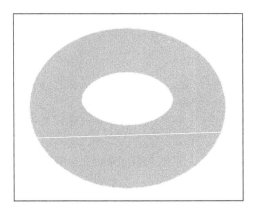

Let there be light!

The flatness is because the scene is lacking light, so let's add light:

```
var light = SCNLight()
light.type = SCNLightTypeSpot
var lightNode = SCNNode()
lightNode.light = light
lightNode.position = SCNVector3(x: 0, y: 0, z: 6)
scene.rootNode.addChildNode(lightNode)
```

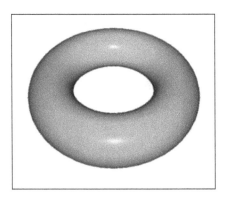

Now the torus definitely looks better.

Let's make it move!

As mentioned earlier, we can apply actions to nodes in the same way as we do in SpriteKit; for example, we can forever move the light to the left and right:

```
let moveAction = SCNAction.sequence([
    SCNAction.moveByX(-2, y: 0, z: 0, duration: 1),
    SCNAction.moveByX(2, y: 0, z: 0, duration: 1),
    SCNAction.moveByX(2, y: 0, z: 0, duration: 1),
    SCNAction.moveByX(-2, y: 0, z: 0, duration: 1)
])
lightNode.runAction(SCNAction.repeatActionForever(moveAction))
```

We can also make the torus rotate:

```
let rotateAction = SCNAction.rotateByAngle(CGFloat(M_PI),
    aroundAxis: SCNVector3(x: 1.0, y: 0.0, z: 0.0),
    duration: 4.0)

torusNode.runAction(SCNAction.repeatActionForever(rotateAction))
```

It's amazing what we can build with just a few lines of code in such an interactive way!

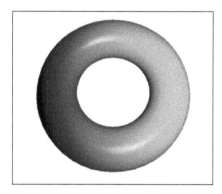

In this brief introduction, we have just scratched the surface of what we can do with SceneKit. Nevertheless, we have introduced the key concepts of SceneKit, which will help us implement our game without any problem.

Implementing Cube Runner

After experimenting a bit with SceneKit, let's start implementing our game.

The game skeleton

As usual, let's start by selecting the correct Xcode project template, the **Game** template in this case, which looks like this:

In the next screen, we add the requested data and select **SceneKit** as the technology, as shown here:

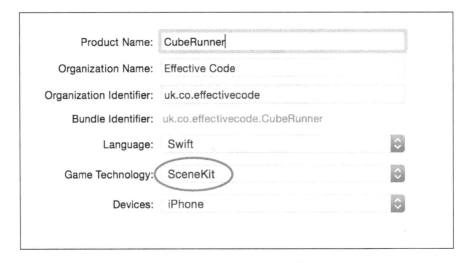

After selecting only **Portrait** as the allowed orientation, as shown in the following screenshot, we can run the example project:

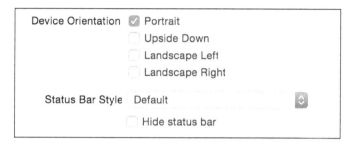

The demo app shows a gorgeous rotating 3D airplane, thus showing us what we can achieve using this framework. Here is a screenshot of the plane:

Implementing the menu

For the first task in building the app, we prepare the Podfile, which contains a few pods that we'll use to build the menu view:

```
inhibit_all_warnings!
use_frameworks!
target 'CubeRunner' do
    pod 'Cartography', '~> 0.5'
    pod 'HTPressableButton', '~> 1.3'
    pod 'BitwiseFont', '~> 0.1.0'
end
```

After running the usual `pod install` command, we are ready to implement the `MenuViewController`.

The code of this class is basically the same as what we used from the previous game, so it shouldn't need any further explanation. First, we need to add the builder to `AppDelegate`:

```
      func application(application: UIApplication,
   didFinishLaunchingWithOptions launchOptions: [NSObject: AnyObject]?)
   -> Bool {
           let viewController = MenuViewController()
           let mainWindow = UIWindow(frame: UIScreen.mainScreen().bounds)
           mainWindow.backgroundColor = UIColor.whiteColor()
           mainWindow.rootViewController = viewController
           mainWindow.makeKeyAndVisible()
           window = mainWindow
           return true
      }
```

Then we implement the ViewController, which presents the menu to select the game sections and a label with the name of the game using a cool font:

```
import UIKit
import HTPressableButton
import Cartography
import BitwiseFont

class MenuViewController: UIViewController {
    private let playButton = HTPressableButton(frame: CGRectMake(0, 0,
260, 50), buttonStyle: .Rect)
    private let gameCenterButton = HTPressableButton(frame:
CGRectMake(0, 0, 260, 50), buttonStyle: .Rect)
    private let titleLbl = UILabel()

    override func viewDidLoad() {
        super.viewDidLoad()
        setup()
        layoutView()
        style()
        render()
    }
}
```

The setup prepares the components and the transitions to other ViewControllers:

```
// MARK: Setup
private extension MenuViewController{
    func setup(){
        playButton.addTarget(self, action: "onPlayPressed:",
forControlEvents: .TouchUpInside)
        view.addSubview(playButton)
        gameCenterButton.addTarget(self, action:
"onGameCenterPressed:", forControlEvents: .TouchUpInside)
        view.addSubview(gameCenterButton)
        view.addSubview(titleLbl)
    }

    @objc func onPlayPressed(sender: UIButton) {
        let vc = GameViewController()
        vc.modalTransitionStyle = .CrossDissolve
        presentViewController(vc, animated: true, completion: nil)
    }

    @objc func onGameCenterPressed(sender: UIButton) {
        println("onGameCenterPressed")
    }
}
```

The components are centered horizontally and placed in the screen to fill it in a uniform way:

```
// MARK: Layout
extension MenuViewController{
    func layoutView() {
        layout(titleLbl) { view in
            view.top == view.superview!.top + 60
            view.centerX == view.superview!.centerX
        }
        layout(playButton) { view in
            view.bottom == view.superview!.centerY - 60
            view.centerX == view.superview!.centerX
            view.height == 80
            view.width == view.superview!.width - 40
        }
        layout(gameCenterButton) { view in
            view.bottom == view.superview!.centerY + 60
            view.centerX == view.superview!.centerX
            view.height == 80
```

```
                view.width == view.superview!.width - 40
            }
        }
    }
```

The `style()` function uses the flat UI colors that the `HTPressableButtons` brought with it:

```
// MARK: Style
private extension MenuViewController{
    func style(){
        playButton.buttonColor = UIColor.ht_grapeFruitColor()
        playButton.shadowColor = UIColor.ht_grapeFruitDarkColor()
        playButton.titleLabel?.font = UIFont.bitwiseFontOfSize(30)
        gameCenterButton.buttonColor = UIColor.ht_aquaColor()
        gameCenterButton.shadowColor = UIColor.ht_aquaDarkColor()
        gameCenterButton.titleLabel?.font = UIFont.
bitwiseFontOfSize(30)
        titleLbl.textColor = UIColor.ht_midnightBlueColor()
        titleLbl.font = UIFont.bitwiseFontOfSize(50)
    }
}
```

Finally, the render inserts the text as the caption of the components:

```
// MARK: Render
private extension MenuViewController{
    func render(){
        playButton.setTitle("Play", forState: .Normal)
        gameCenterButton.setTitle("Game Center", forState: .Normal)
        titleLbl.text = "Cube Runner"
    }
}
```

Run the app. The menu has a fancy retro taste, as shown in this screenshot:

 You can find the code for this version at `https://github.com/gscalzo/CubeRunner/tree/menu`.

Flying in a 3D world

Let's now build a scene where we can fly, by skipping colorful cubes.

Setting up the scene

By running the app built so far, you might have noticed that on selecting the **Play** button, the app crashes. This is because `GameViewController` expects to be set up by the storyboard where the view is actually an `SCNView`, and because the view is a plain `UIView`, it crashes.

To fix this issue, we need to build a slim `GameViewController` from scratch:

```
import UIKit
import QuartzCore
import SceneKit

class GameViewController: UIViewController {
    private let scnView = SCNView()
    private var scene: SCNScene!

    override func viewDidLoad() {
```

```
        super.viewDidLoad()
        scnView.frame = view.bounds
        view.addSubview(scnView)

        createContents()
    }
    override func prefersStatusBarHidden() -> Bool {
        return true
    }
}
```

The `createContents()` function creates all the elements of the game, and it'll be handy to have it as a separate function when we need to implement the restart feature:

```
// MARK: content builder
private extension GameViewController {
    func createContents() {
        scene = SCNScene()
    scnView.showsStatistics = true
        scnView.scene = scene
    }
}
```

Now the game doesn't crash anymore, but the game controller presents a plain white view.

The first node we create is the camera node. We need it to observe the scene. Because we'll need to apply an action to the camera, let's save it as instance variable:

```
class GameViewController: UIViewController {
    //...
    private var cameraNode: SCNNode!
    //...
```

Then in `createContents()`, we create and add it to the scene:

```
    func createContents() {
        //...
        cameraNode = createCamera()
        scene.rootNode.addChildNode(cameraNode)
        scnView.scene = scene
    }
```

The function that creates the node is really straightforward. It just enters the expected position and the correct rotation pointing to the center:

```
func createCamera() -> SCNNode{
    let cameraNode = SCNNode()
    cameraNode.camera = SCNCamera()
    cameraNode.position = SCNVector3Make(0, 7, 20)
    cameraNode.rotation = SCNVector4Make(1, 0, 0, -atan2f(7,
20.0))
    return cameraNode
}
```

The code presented in `createCamera()` is basic trigonometry. The only unusual notation is the one for rotation, where we first define the axis around which we want to rotate the object, **X** in this case. Then we define the angle of rotation; `atan2(y, x)` is the angle in radians between the positive *x* axis of a plane and the point given by the `(x, y)` coordinates on it. The value of this angle is positive for counterclockwise angles (upper half-plane; *y* > 0), and negative for clockwise angles (lower half-plane; *y* < 0).

If you recall the diagram of the coordinates you saw earlier, it should not be difficult to imagine where the camera is, but the following diagram should also help you visualize it:

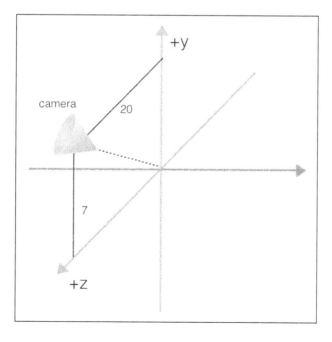

Adding the fighter

A powerful feature of SceneKit is that it can import a 3D scene model exported in COLLADA, which is a royalty-free XML form for the interchange of 3D models.

This means that a graphic artist can create a scene using their usual tools, such as Maya or Blender. Then a developer imports the file into the iOS app without any need for further processing phases.

Moreover, this format opens the doors to be able to use models that can be bought or downloaded for free from a marketplace, such as http://www.turbosquid.com. Indeed, from that marketplace, we'll use a royalty-free jet fighter model that fits the mood of our game perfectly.

Looking at the project window, we notice that there is a folder called art. scnassets, where we must put the 3D assets. This folder is mapped to the filesystem of the project. This means that there is a directory with the same name in the filesystem of the project, and by adding a file to that directory, the file is automatically added to the project.

Let's download the model and add it to the project.

 The model can be downloaded from https://github.com/ gscalzo/CubeRunner/blob/master/assets/model/ eurofighter.dae.zip?raw=true.

By selecting **jetfighter**, as shown in the following screenshot, we can see what compounds the scene:

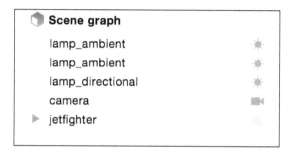

The scene components are different types of light, a camera, and the jet fighter.

We can play with each of them, changing position, materials, and so on. The result will be rendered in the right panel of the screen, like this:

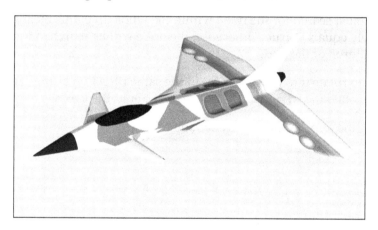

Now that we have added the model of the scene to the project, let's add it to the game.

First of all, instead of creating an empty SCNScene, we need to load the scene from the model:

```
func createContents() {
    scene = SCNScene(named: "art.scnassets/eurofighter.dae")
    scnView.showsStatistics = true
    //...
```

Then we search for the `jetfighter` object, change its size to fit into our scene, and place it between the camera and the center:

```
        let jetfighterNode = createJetfighter()
        scnView.scene = scene
}

    func createJetfighter() -> SCNNode{
        let jetfighterNode = scene!.rootNode.
childNodeWithName("jetfighter", recursively: true)!

        jetfighterNode.scale = SCNVector3(x: 0.03, y: 0.03, z: 0.03)
        jetfighterNode.position = SCNVector3(x: 0, y: 1.0, z: 13)
        jetfighterNode.rotation = SCNVector4(x: 0, y: 1, z: 0, w:
Float(M_PI))
        return jetfighterNode
    }
```

Note that we must search for the node within the whole tree, this means we must user recursively equals to true. Otherwise, the node will be searched for, only in the immediate children of the node.

We also need to rotate it to make it point in the same direction as the camera; to do this, we must rotate the jet fighter by 180 degrees about the y axis.

Upon running the app, we can finally see something:

Texturing the world

A texture is an image that can be added to the surface of a 3D model, making it more realistic. We have already used a texture to add a skin to the jet fighter.

Now we'll add textures to the sky and the floor.

 The images for this purpose can be downloaded from `https://github.com/gscalzo/CubeRunner/blob/master/assets/images/images.zip?raw=true`.

Add the icon and the two images, paying attention to set them as **2x** in their respective panels.

First of all, we set the sky as the texture for the background of the scene:

```
func createContents() {
    scene = SCNScene(named: "art.scnassets/eurofighter.dae")
    scene.background.contents = UIImage(named: "sky")
    scnView.showsStatistics = true
    //...
```

Then we add a special node, `SCNFloor`. It acts as the base of the scene:

```
func createContents() {
//...
let jetfighterNode = createJetfighter()
    scene.rootNode.addChildNode(createFloor())
    //...
```

The `createFloor()` basically creates a floor and applies a texture on top:

```
func createFloor() -> SCNNode {
    let floor = SCNFloor()
    floor.firstMaterial!.diffuse.contents = UIImage(named: "moon")
    floor.firstMaterial!.diffuse.contentsTransform =
SCNMatrix4MakeScale(2, 2, 1)

    floor.reflectivity = 0
    return SCNNode(geometry: floor)
}
```

To apply the texture in the correct place and with the correct scale, we move it using a transformation of its coordinates — `floor.firstMaterial!.diffuse.contentsTransform`.

Now the app has started looking like a real game:

Make it move

As we have already seen in the introduction, applying actions to nodes is really straightforward. So, making the jet fighter fly on the moon is just a matter of adding an action to make the camera, and the fighter itself, move towards the horizon:

```
func createContents() {
    //...
    let moveForwardAction = SCNAction.repeatActionForever(
        SCNAction.moveByX(0, y: 0, z: -100, duration: 7))
        cameraNode.runAction(moveForwardAction)
        jetfighterNode.runAction(moveForwardAction)
        //...
        scnView.scene = scene
```

Obviously, the speed can be tweaked and can also be selected, depending on the level of difficulty.

To pilot the jet, we'll use a motion detector so that the plane will respond to the rotation of the iPhone by the player. The first thing we need to do is to import `CoreMotion`:

```
import SceneKit
import CoreMotion
```

We need to save the `motionManager` variable that we'll create in a property:

```
class GameViewController: UIViewController {
//...
    private var motionManager : CMMotionManager?
```

In `createContents()`, we create the `coreManager` object and set the closure that will be called at every change in position of the iPhone:

```
    func createContents() {
//...
        motionManager = CMMotionManager()
        motionManager?.deviceMotionUpdateInterval = 1.0 / 60.0
        motionManager?.startDeviceMotionUpdatesUsingReferenceFrame(
            CMAttitudeReferenceFrame.XArbitraryZVertical,
            toQueue: NSOperationQueue.mainQueue(),
            withHandler: { (motion: CMDeviceMotion!, error: NSError!)
-> Void in
                let roll = CGFloat(motion.attitude.roll)

                let rotateCamera =
                SCNAction.rotateByAngle(roll/20.0,
                                        aroundAxis: SCNVector3(x: 0,
y: 0, z: 1),
                                        duration: 0.1)
                self.cameraNode.runAction(rotateCamera)

                let rotateJetfighter =
                SCNAction.rotateByAngle(roll/10.0,
                                        aroundAxis: SCNVector3(x: 0,
y: 0, z: 1),
                                        duration: 0.1)
                jetfighterNode.runAction(rotateJetfighter)

                let actionMove = SCNAction.moveByX(roll, y: 0, z: 0,
duration: 0.1)
```

```
                self.cameraNode.runAction(actionMove)
                jetfighterNode.runAction(actionMove)
        })
        //...
```

We are getting the value of roll, which is the rotation around the vertical axis of the physical iPhone when it is in portrait mode. We use the retrieved value to move and rotate the camera and jet fighter accordingly.

Because we want to add more visual feedback to the game, we must have the jet rotating more than the camera, so we need to create two different actions for the rotation. One of them will have a greater angle of rotation than the other.

All of these values are calculated using trial and error, and by running the app to see how they change the animation. You can change these values to experiment and better understand how these things work.

 You can find the code for this version at `https://github.com/gscalzo/CubeRunner/tree/plain_scene`.

Adding the cubes

In the original game, sections of random cubes are interleaved with sections of an elaborated path.

For simplicity, our version will present a smooth, curved path that repeats itself in a section of 200 steps.

To create the path, we need to calculate a cubic spline, which is a curve that connects several points smoothly.

To do this, we'll use the `SwiftCubicSpline` pod, which creates a curve like this one:

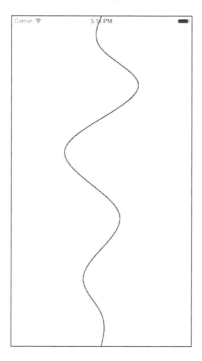

Because it's a pod, it is straightforward to use; just add this to the Podfile:

```
pod 'SwiftCubicSpline', '~> 0.1.0'
```

After running the `pod install` command, we are ready to use the cubic spline interpolation to create a path. Let's import the framework and create a constant spline:

```swift
import SwiftCubicSpline
class GameViewController: UIViewController {
  //...
  private let spline = CubicSpline(points: [
        CGPoint(x: 0.0, y: 0.5),
        CGPoint(x: 0.1, y: 0.5),
        CGPoint(x: 0.2, y: 0.8),
        CGPoint(x: 0.4, y: 0.2),
        CGPoint(x: 0.6, y: 0.6),
        CGPoint(x: 0.8, y: 0.4),
        CGPoint(x: 0.9, y: 0.5),
        CGPoint(x: 1.0, y: 0.5)
        ])
   //...
```

In `createContents()`, after creating the `motionManager`, we call the function to create the first section of the lane:

```
func createContents() {
//...
motionManager?.startDeviceMotionUpdatesUsingReferenceFrame(
        //...
    })
        buildTheLane()
        //...
```

This function just iterates for each step of the section and calls another function to create the actual piece of the lane:

```
func buildTheLane() {
    for var zPos = 0; zPos < 200; zPos += 3 {
        let z = cameraNode.position.z - Float(zPos)
        buildCubesAtPosition(z)
    }
}
```

The `buildCubesAtPosition()` function is a little more complicated:

```
func buildCubesAtPosition(zPos: Float){
    let laneWidth: CGFloat = 40

    let zPosInSection = zPos%200
    let normalizedZ = CGFloat(fabs(zPosInSection/200))
    let normalizedX = Float((spline.interpolate(normalizedZ) -
0.5)*laneWidth)

    var cubeAtLeft = cube()
    cubeAtLeft.position = SCNVector3(x: normalizedX - 6, y: 1.0,
z: zPos)
    scene.rootNode.addChildNode(cubeAtLeft)
    var cubeAtRight = cube()
    cubeAtRight.position = SCNVector3(x: normalizedX + 6, y: 1.0,
z: zPos)
    scene.rootNode.addChildNode(cubeAtRight)
}
```

First, we get the position inside the current section. Then, because the spline is in the 0–1 range, we normalize the position to be in the same range.

Given the normalized value, we calculate the *x* position in the spline and denormalize again to create a position that is within the coordinates of the screen.

The position we have just calculated is central with respect to the screen, but we need two values for each of the cubes that creates the lane. Given the width of the lane of 12 steps, we set the cubes at each side:

```
func cube(size: CGFloat = 2.0) -> SCNNode {
    let cube = SCNBox(width: size, height: size, length: size,
chamferRadius: 0)
    let cubeNode = SCNNode(geometry: cube)

    cube.firstMaterial!.diffuse.contents = {
        switch arc4random_uniform(4) {
        case 0:
            return UIColor.ht_belizeHoleColor()
        case 1:
            return UIColor.ht_wisteriaColor()
        case 2:
            return UIColor.ht_midnightBlueColor()
        default:
            return UIColor.ht_pomegranateColor()
        }
    }()

    return cubeNode
}
```

The cube() function uses a primitive function of SceneKit to create a cube and set a random color for its face. Notice how we have created an anonymous function and then called it in place, to wrap the logic of selecting a random color.

The game is now pretty cool!

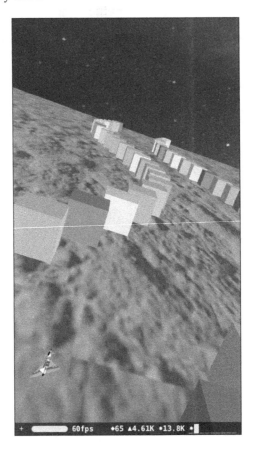

However, we have just created the first section; we need to create an infinite lane. To do this, we set a timer that creates a piece of lane every 1/5th of a second.

As we might need to invalidate the timer, we create a property for it:

```
class GameViewController: UIViewController {
//...
    private var laneTimer: NSTimer!
```

Then we set up the timer in `createContents()`:

```
    func createContents() {
//...
buildTheLane()
        laneTimer = NSTimer.scheduledTimerWithTimeInterval(0.2,
target: self,
            selector: "laneTimerFired", userInfo: nil, repeats: true)
```

Since the section is 200 steps long, we need to build a piece of lane 200 steps in front of the camera in the callback called when the timer fires:

```
    @objc func laneTimerFired(){
        buildCubesAtPosition(cameraNode.position.z-200)
    }
```

If you run the app now, you will find that the lane is endless and it allows the player to race for a longer run.

However, there's still a small glitch that makes our game not so believable: we can see the cubes of the lane being built, popping up on the horizon. To fix this issue, we use a nice feature of SceneKit: the fog at a long distance. In our case, it will be black to simulate the night:

```
    func createContents() {
//...
laneTimer = NSTimer.scheduledTimerWithTimeInterval(0.2, target: self,
            selector: "laneTimerFired", userInfo: nil, repeats: true)
        scene!.fogStartDistance = 30
        scene!.fogEndDistance = 90
        scene!.fogColor = UIColor.blackColor()
```

By running the app now, we can see a nice night-like effect on the horizon, which seems as if the cubes appear from the darker side of the moon, like this:

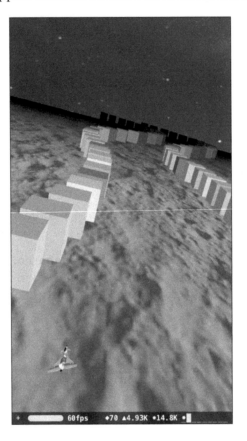

Adding more obstacles

Although we haven't completed the game yet—notably, collision detection is missing—we can already see that the game is too easy to play. One way to increase the difficulty of the path is to add a few cubes inside the path:

```
func buildCubesAtPosition(zPos: Float){
    //...
    if arc4random_uniform(5) < 1 {
        var centralCube = cube(size: 1.0)
        scene.rootNode.addChildNode(centralCube)
        let xOffset = arc4random_uniform(10)
        centralCube.position = SCNVector3(x: normalizedX +
Float(xOffset) - 5.0, y: 1.0, z: zPos)
    }
}
```

This code is added to the function that is responsible for building the lane when a certain *z* position is given. Using `arc4random_uniform(5)`, there is a one-out-of-five probability of placing a small cube in every piece of the lane. In this way, the game can never be exactly the same as before.

The position of the cube inside the lane is random as well. Although collision detection is still missing, the game is already fun to play with.

 You can find the code for this version at `https://github.com/` `gscalzo/CubeRunner/tree/cubes`.

Adding a few touches

Although a few things are still missing, either some parts of them are straightforward or we have already implemented them in the previous chapters when we were building Flappy Swift.

The score

The score falls under the straightforward category, and it is worthwhile implementing it right now, so we can finish adding all the visual elements to the screen.

The goal of the game is for the player to keep going as long as they can without colliding with a cube. So to implement the score, we just need to schedule a timer that fires every second, increasing the score. First of all, we need to add the elements as properties:

```
class GameViewController: UIViewController {
    //...
    private var laneTimer: NSTimer!
    private let scoreLbl = UILabel()
    private var scoreTimer: NSTimer!
    private var score = 0
```

Then we set up the score, calling `setupScore()` in `createContents()`:

```
func createContents() {
//...
        scene!.fogColor = UIColor.blackColor()
        setupScore()
        //...
    }
```

The `setupScore()` function adds the label to the `Views` hierarchy and sets the correct style:

```
func setupScore() {
    scnView.addSubview(scoreLbl)
    scoreLbl.frame.origin.x = 0
    scoreLbl.frame.origin.y = 0
    scoreLbl.frame.size.height = 50
    scoreLbl.frame.size.width = 200
    scoreLbl.font = UIFont.bitwiseFontOfSize(30)
    scoreLbl.textColor = UIColor.whiteColor()
    score = 0
    scoreLbl.text = "\(score)"
```

```
        scoreTimer = NSTimer.scheduledTimerWithTimeInterval(1, target:
    self, selector: "scoreTimerFired", userInfo: nil, repeats: true)
        }
```

Finally, the closure bound to the `scoreTimer` increases the score and sets the value in the label:

```
    @objc func scoreTimerFired(){
        score++
        scoreLbl.text = "\(score)"
    }
```

The game now presents a fancy score in the top-left corner, with a juicy retro font.

Let's add the music

The music falls under the *already implemented* category, and we can reuse the
MusicPlayer class we created for Flappy Swift:

```
import Foundation
import AVFoundation

class MusicPlayer {
    private let player: AVAudioPlayer?

    init(filename: String, type: String){
        if let resource = NSBundle.mainBundle().
pathForResource(filename, ofType: type) {
            let url = NSURL(fileURLWithPath: resource)
            player = AVAudioPlayer(contentsOfURL: url, error: nil);
            player!.numberOfLoops = -1
            player!.prepareToPlay()
        }
    }

    func play() {
        if let player = player {
            player.play()
        }
    }
    func stop() {
        if let player = player {
            player.stop()
        }
    }
}
```

For the soundtrack, we rely again on Kevin MacLeod and his website at
http://incompetech.com. We use a calm space song called *Space 1990-B*.

 The soundtrack file can be downloaded from https://github.
com/gscalzo/CubeRunner/blob/master/assets/music/
Space%201990-B.mp3?raw=true.

Let's add `musicPlayer` as a property:

```
class GameViewController: UIViewController {
  //...
    private let musicPlayer = MusicPlayer(filename: "Space 1990-B",
              type: "mp3")
    //...
```

Then implement `viewWillAppear()` and `viewDidDisappear()` to start and stop the music respectively:

```
override func viewWillAppear(animated: Bool) {
    super.viewWillAppear(animated)
    musicPlayer.play()
}
override func viewDidDisappear(animated: Bool) {
    super.viewDidDisappear(animated)
    musicPlayer.stop()
}
```

That's it! As already mentioned, although not finished, the game still looks complete and fun.

 You can find the code for this version at `https://github.com/gscalzo/FlappySwift/tree/music_score`.

Summary

The aim of this chapter was to introduce SceneKit, demystifying the idea that 3D game development is something that only professional game developers can do. We showed you how Playground can help you learn about a new library, for example, SceneKit. This allows you to build and modify nodes when they are shown in the console of Playground.

Then we began implementing a complete 3D game, and although it is not done yet, we have almost created a prototype—a game that, in real life, could be enough to start playing, and share with other players, to gather feedback and steer its development in the correct direction.

In the following chapter, we'll carry on with the development of this game by adding the missing features, notably one feature that could make the game look gorgeous—explosions!

8
Completing Cube Runner

In the previous chapter, we implemented most of the features of Cube Runner. In this chapter, we will finish implementing the game.

The most notable feature that is missing is collision detection, so we'll start with that in this chapter. As we have already said, when we built Flappy Swift, Game Center support made the game more interesting, so we'll add that to Cube Runner as well.

Let's get started with all of this, and much more, in this chapter.

Making it a real game

The first thing we must implement to make this a real game is collision detection. Then we'll add an end to the game, otherwise it will be really boring. Finally, the usual *juiciness* will make the game more appealing.

Detecting collisions

Collision detection in SceneKit is implemented as it is in SpriteKit. For every node that can collide, we must create a physics body and attach it to the node, setting a unique identifier for that body. Finally, a contact delegate will receive a call when a collision is detected.

First of all, we define an enumeration to list all the possible types of bodies, which are only two in our case:

```
enum BodyType : Int {
    case jetfighter = 1  // (1 << 0)
    case cube       = 2  // (1 << 1)
}
```

In `createJetfighter()`, we create a parallelepiped to act as a physics body for the jet fighter, because using the actual model we used for rendering is a waste of calculation resources. For the purpose of detecting a collision, a rough shape is enough:

```
func createJetfighter() -> SCNNode{
    //...
    let jetfighterBodyNode = SCNNode(geometry:
        SCNBox(width: 0.3, height: 0.2, length: 1, chamferRadius:
0))
    jetfighterNode.physicsBody = SCNPhysicsBody(type: .Kinematic,
shape:
    SCNPhysicsShape(node: jetfighterBodyNode, options: nil))
    jetfighterNode.physicsBody!.categoryBitMask = BodyType.
jetfighter.rawValue
    jetfighterNode.physicsBody!.collisionBitMask = BodyType.cube.
rawValue

    return jetfighterNode
}
```

We create the already mentioned parallelepiped, which is of the `jetfighter` type, as by the category bitmask, and it collides with a cube, as by the collision bitmask.

We can do a similar thing for cubes:

```
func cube(size: CGFloat = 2.0) -> SCNNode {
//...
    let cubeNode = SCNNode(geometry: cube)
    cubeNode.physicsBody = SCNPhysicsBody(type: .Static, shape:
SCNPhysicsShape(node: cubeNode, options: nil))
    cubeNode.physicsBody!.categoryBitMask = BodyType.cube.rawValue
    cubeNode.physicsBody!.collisionBitMask = BodyType.jetfighter.
rawValue
    //...
}
```

Although the code is the same, the category and collision bitmasks are the other way round. Finally, we must assign the `GameViewController` class as `contactDelegate`:

```
func createContents() {
    scene = SCNScene(named: "art.scnassets/eurofighter.dae")
    scene.physicsWorld.contactDelegate = self
//...
```

Obviously, we must implement that protocol, and we do it in a similar way to how we did for Flappy Swift:

```
extension GameViewController: SCNPhysicsContactDelegate{
    func physicsWorld(world: SCNPhysicsWorld,
        didBeginContact contact: SCNPhysicsContact){
            let contactMask = contact.nodeA.physicsBody!.
categoryBitMask | contact.nodeB.physicsBody!.categoryBitMask
            switch (contactMask) {
            case BodyType.jetfighter.rawValue |  BodyType.cube.
rawValue:
                println("Contact!")
            default:
                return
            }

        }
}
```

Run the app to verify that everything works as expected, as shown here:

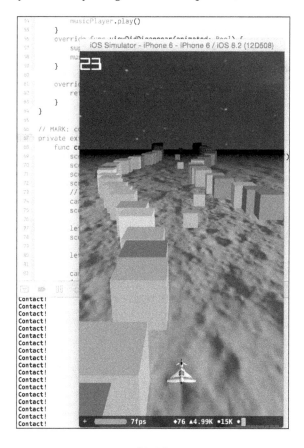

Game Over!

When the jet fighter touches a cube, we must do a few things to stop everything from moving, such as invalidate the timers, remove all the actions of the nodes, disable the CoreMotion manager, and so on.

This means that all of these objects must be accessible through the delegate method. To do this, we will put `jetfighterNode` as an instance variable, but to reduce the quantity of code, we must change this. We create a property to hold the function that will be called in the delegate method. That function wraps the value of `jetfighterNode` so that we don't need to transform it into an instance variable.

First of all, we define the property:

```
class GameViewController: UIViewController {
    //...
    private var gameOver: () -> Void = {}
```

The function will be a function without any arguments and return values. Then in `createContents()`, we assign the function's body:

```
func createContents() {
  //...
    setupScore()
    gameOver = { [unowned self] in
        self.laneTimer.invalidate()
        self.scoreTimer.invalidate()
        self.scene.physicsWorld.contactDelegate = nil
        self.cameraNode.removeAllActions()
        jetfighterNode.removeAllActions()
        self.motionManager?.stopDeviceMotionUpdates()
    }
```

As you can see, the body of the function is nothing more than the statements meant to stop everything.

Finally, we call the function after contact:

```
func physicsWorld(world: SCNPhysicsWorld,
    didBeginContact contact: SCNPhysicsContact){
        //..
case BodyType.jetfighter.rawValue |
BodyType.cube.rawValue:
            println("Contact!")
    gameOver()
```

By running the app, we see that the game stops when the jet fighter touches a cube—precisely what we were expecting. However, the only way to play again is by killing and restarting the app, which is not exactly convenient.

We need to implement a way of restarting the game. To do that, we'll use the `SIAlertView` pod to ask the player whether they want to play again or whether they want to go back to the menu view.

First, we update the Podfile by adding this pod:

```
pod 'SIAlertView', '~> 1.3'
```

After installing the pods with `pod install`, we import the framework:

```
//...
import SwiftCubicSpline
import SIAlertView
```

We can now create a function to present the alert dialog:

```
func askToPlayAgain(#onPlayAgainPressed: () -> Void,
    onCancelPressed: () -> Void) {
        let alertView = SIAlertView(title: "Ouch!!", andMessage:
"Congratulations! Your score is \(score). Play again?")

        alertView.addButtonWithTitle("OK", type: .Default) { _ in
onPlayAgainPressed() }
        alertView.addButtonWithTitle("Cancel", type: .Default) { _ in
onCancelPressed() }
        alertView.show()
}
```

As you can see, depending on which button is pressed, either of the functions passed as parameters are called. The functions are defined in the `gameOver()` function:

```
        gameOver = { [unowned self] in
//...
            self.motionManager?.stopDeviceMotionUpdates()
            self.askToPlayAgain(onPlayAgainPressed: {
                self.createContents()
                return
            },
            onCancelPressed: {
                self.dismissViewControllerAnimated(true,
completion: nil)
                return
            }
            )
        }
```

The first function calls the `createContents()` function to restart the game, and now it is clear that it wasn't only a readability issue because of which we grouped together the creation statements in a new function.

The second function dismisses the ViewController to go back to `MenuViewController`. If we run the app now, it seems as if everything works as expected, but the popup is slightly delayed.

By putting a breakpoint in the body of the `gameOver()` function and running the debugger, we notice that the function is not called in the main thread, but in the rendering thread, as shown in this screenshot:

The problem is that every change to the UI must be done in the main thread, otherwise unexpected things—even crashes—can happen. What a rookie mistake!

This issue is easy to fix; create a convenience function to run a closure in the main thread:

```
func execInMainThread(closure:()->()) {
    dispatch_async(dispatch_get_main_queue(),closure)
}
```

In the `gameOver()` function, we wrap the call to `SIAlertView` using the previous function:

```
        gameOver = { [unowned self] in
//...
            self.motionManager?.stopDeviceMotionUpdates()
            execInMainThread(){
                self.askToPlayAgain(onPlayAgainPressed: {
                    self.createContents()
                    return
                },
                onCancelPressed: {
                    self.dismissViewControllerAnimated(true,
completion: nil)
                    return
                }
                )
            }
        }
```

Finally, everything works as expected.

Adding the juice

As mentioned in the previous chapters, adding a few touches can change a game from plain to juicy.

Because the game is controlled using the motion of an iPhone, it is always in the hands of the player, so it will be nice to receive tactile feedback when the jet fighter crashes into a cube.

This can be easily implemented using vibrations, which can be triggered programmatically using a service of `AudioToolbox`. Let's import the framework:

```
//...
import SIAlertView
import AudioToolbox.AudioServices
```

Then add a function call to `gameOver()`:

```
gameOver = { [unowned self] in
  //...
  self.motionManager?.stopDeviceMotionUpdates()          AudioServices
  PlayAlertSound(SystemSoundID(kSystemSoundID_Vibrate))
```

A nice feature provided by SceneKit is a particle engine, which allows us to use a large number of small sprites to simulate certain fuzzy phenomena, such as fire, smoke, explosions, and so on.

First of all, let's add the `FireParticles.scnp` particle file and the `spark.png` sprite image to the project.

 You can find the resources at `https://github.com/gscalzo/CubeRunner/tree/master/assets/explosion`.

Upon selecting the particle file, you will notice that you can tweak its value, and Xcode presents the result in a nice console view, like this:

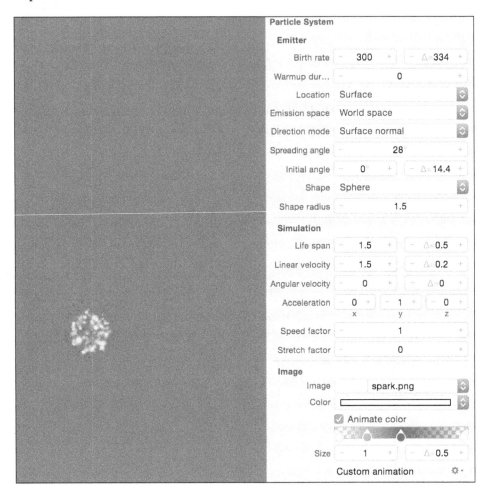

The idea is to make both the jet fighter and the cube explode when the former hits the latter. Let's create a function to add a particle system to a node:

```
func explodeNode(node: SCNNode){
    let fire = SCNParticleSystem(named: "FireParticles",
inDirectory: nil)
    fire.emitterShape = node.geometry
    node.addParticleSystem(fire)
}
```

As you can see, adding a particle system is really straightforward. However, we need to change the gameOver() signature to pass the two nodes:

```
class GameViewController: UIViewController {
  //...
    private var gameOver: (SCNNode, SCNNode) -> Void = {_,_ in}
```

Then we change the body of gameOver():

```
gameOver = { [unowned self] nodeA, nodeB in
  //...
    self.cameraNode.removeAllActions()
    jetfighterNode.removeAllActions()
    self.explodeNode(nodeA)
    self.explodeNode(nodeB)
  //...
}
```

Finally, we change the call of the gameOver() function:

```
func physicsWorld(world: SCNPhysicsWorld,
    didBeginContact contact: SCNPhysicsContact){
        //..
  case BodyType.jetfighter.rawValue |
    BodyType.cube.rawValue:
        gameOver(contact.nodeA, contact.nodeB)
```

To give the player a chance to see the jet fighter and the cube burning before being covered by the popup, we delay the appearance of the popup. From previous apps, we copy execAfter():

```
func execAfter(delay:Double, closure:()->()) {
    dispatch_after(
        dispatch_time(
            DISPATCH_TIME_NOW,
            Int64(delay * Double(NSEC_PER_SEC))
        ),
        dispatch_get_main_queue(), closure)
}
```

Then we replace in gameOver() the execInMainThreat() call to execAfter(), using 1 second as the delay:

```
gameOver = { [unowned self] nodeA, nodeB in
            self.laneTimer.invalidate()
//...
            AudioServicesPlayAlertSound(
```

```
SystemSoundID(kSystemSoundID_Vibrate))
            execAfter(1){
                self.askToPlayAgain(onPlayAgainPressed: {
```

Nice, isn't it?

 You can find the code for this version at `https://github.com/gscalzo/CubeRunner/tree/playable_game`.

Game Center

The last thing that is missing is integration with Game Center. We'll use the code we had written for Flappy Swift for this purpose.

You might remember that there is a tedious series of operations to be done on the Apple backend servers. In order not to waste pages duplicating information, the procedure described in *Chapter 6, Polishing Flappy Swift*, can be referred to.

After setting up the leaderboard and the test user, we can copy the GameCenter class we created for Flappy Swift:

```swift
import GameKit
import SIAlertView

class GameCenter: NSObject {
    private var gameCenterEnabled = false
    private var leaderboardIdentifier = ""

    func authenticateLocalPlayer() {
        let localPlayer = GKLocalPlayer.localPlayer()
        localPlayer.authenticateHandler = { (viewController, error) in
            if let vc = viewController {
                let topViewController = UIApplication.
sharedApplication().delegate!.window!!.rootViewController
                topViewController?.presentViewController(vc, animated:
true, completion: nil)
            } else if localPlayer.authenticated {
                self.gameCenterEnabled = true
                localPlayer.
loadDefaultLeaderboardIdentifierWithCompletionHandler({
(leaderboardIdentifier, error) -> Void in
                    self.leaderboardIdentifier = leaderboardIdentifier
                })
            }
        }
    }

    func reportScore(score: Int){
        if !gameCenterEnabled {
            return
        }

        let gkScore = GKScore(leaderboardIdentifier:
leaderboardIdentifier)
```

```
        gkScore.value = Int64(score)

        GKScore.reportScores([gkScore], withCompletionHandler: nil)
    }



    func showLeaderboard() {
        if !gameCenterEnabled {
            let alertView = SIAlertView(title: "Game Center
Unavailable", andMessage: "Player is not signed in")

            alertView.addButtonWithTitle("OK", type: .Default) { _ in
    }
            alertView.show()
            return
        }


    let gcViewController = GKGameCenterViewController()

    gcViewController.gameCenterDelegate = self
    gcViewController.viewState = .Leaderboards
    gcViewController.leaderboardIdentifier = leaderboardIdentifier

        let topViewController = UIApplication.sharedApplication().
delegate!.window!!.rootViewController
        topViewController?.presentViewController(gcViewController,
animated: true, completion: nil)
        }
}

extension GameCenter: GKGameCenterControllerDelegate {
    func gameCenterViewControllerDidFinish(gameCenterViewController:
GKGameCenterViewController){
        gameCenterViewController.dismissViewControllerAnimated(true,
completion: nil)
        }
}
```

Just a reminder of what this class is for: GameCenter is a wrapper class around the Game Center functionalities. It provides three features:

- **Authentication**: Through the authenticateLocalPlayer() function, the class permits logging automatically or shows a form with a username and a password

- **Reporting score**: The reportScore() function wraps the call to the Game Center server to send the current score

- **Showing the leaderboard**: The showLeaderboard() function opens a new view with the leaderboard, or fails with an alert dialog if the player is not logged in

Once again, we set up the GameCenter class in MenuViewController:

```
class MenuViewController: UIViewController {
    //...
    private let gameCenter = GameCenter()
    override func viewDidLoad() {
        super.viewDidLoad()
        gameCenter.authenticateLocalPlayer()
    //...
Then we call showLeaderboard() in the callback of the Game Center
button:
    @objc func onGameCenterPressed(sender: UIButton) {
        println("onGameCenterPressed")
        gameCenter.showLeaderboard()
    }
Finally, we need to pass the instance of GameCenter to the
GameViewController class:
    @objc func onPlayPressed(sender: UIButton) {
        let vc = GameViewController()
        vc.gameCenter = gameCenter
        //...
    }
```

In this class, we add a property to hold the instance of GameCenter:

```
class GameViewController: UIViewController {
    //...
    private var gameOver: (SCNNode, SCNNode) -> Void = {_,_ in}
    var gameCenter: GameCenter?
```

The score, which is in the body of gameOver(), is sent to the server when the game ends:

```
gameOver = { [unowned self] nodeA, nodeB in
  //...
  self.motionManager?.stopDeviceMotionUpdates()
    if let gameCenter = self.gameCenter{
        gameCenter.reportScore(self.score)
    }
    //...
```

Finally, we have completed the game and we are ready to challenge our friends on the longest run between the cubes.

 You can find the code for this version at `https://github.com/gscalzo/CubeRunner/tree/game_center`.

Summary

This chapter was shorter than most of the others in this book. Nevertheless, we finished building the Cube Runner game by adding a proper game over feature, explosions, and a vibration in the case of a crash with a cube. We set up Game Center to collect the scores.

Although the game is pretty fun, there's always room for improvement; for example, different lanes could easily be added, or you could put different building functions for every section. You might even want to change the texture and shape of the cube to create planets. A bullet shooting from the jet could be added to wipe out some small cubes inside the lanes.

However, adding these enhancements could be challenging. Nevertheless, you must have a good amount of knowledge of Swift and the frameworks by now — enough to start developing iOS apps in Swift on your own.

Index

Symbols

Thank you for buying
Swift by Example

About Packt Publishing

Packt, pronounced 'packed', published its first book, *Mastering phpMyAdmin for Effective MySQL Management*, in April 2004, and subsequently continued to specialize in publishing highly focused books on specific technologies and solutions.

Our books and publications share the experiences of your fellow IT professionals in adapting and customizing today's systems, applications, and frameworks. Our solution-based books give you the knowledge and power to customize the software and technologies you're using to get the job done. Packt books are more specific and less general than the IT books you have seen in the past. Our unique business model allows us to bring you more focused information, giving you more of what you need to know, and less of what you don't.

Packt is a modern yet unique publishing company that focuses on producing quality, cutting-edge books for communities of developers, administrators, and newbies alike. For more information, please visit our website at www.packtpub.com.

About Packt Open Source

In 2010, Packt launched two new brands, Packt Open Source and Packt Enterprise, in order to continue its focus on specialization. This book is part of the Packt Open Source brand, home to books published on software built around open source licenses, and offering information to anybody from advanced developers to budding web designers. The Open Source brand also runs Packt's Open Source Royalty Scheme, by which Packt gives a royalty to each open source project about whose software a book is sold.

Writing for Packt

We welcome all inquiries from people who are interested in authoring. Book proposals should be sent to author@packtpub.com. If your book idea is still at an early stage and you would like to discuss it first before writing a formal book proposal, then please contact us; one of our commissioning editors will get in touch with you.

We're not just looking for published authors; if you have strong technical skills but no writing experience, our experienced editors can help you develop a writing career, or simply get some additional reward for your expertise.

Swift Essentials

ISBN: 978-1-78439-670-1   Paperback: 228 pages

Get up and running lightning fast with this practical guide to building applications with Swift

1. Rapidly learn how to program Apple's newest programming language, Swift, from the basics through to working applications.

2. Create graphical iOS applications using Xcode and storyboard.

3. Build a network client for GitHub repositories, with full source code on GitHub.

iOS 5 Essentials

ISBN: 978-1-84969-226-7   Paperback: 252 pages

Harness iOS 5's new powerful features to create stunning applications

1. Integrate iCloud, Twitter and AirPlay into your applications.

2. Lots of step-by-step examples, images and diagrams to get you up to speed in no time with helpful hints along the way.

3. Each chapter explains iOS 5's new features in-depth, whilst providing you with enough practical examples to help incorporate these features in your apps.

iOS Development with Xamarin Cookbook

ISBN: 978-1-84969-892-4   Paperback: 386 pages

Over 100 exciting recipes to help you develop iOS applications with Xamarin

1. Explore the new features of Xamarin and learn how to use them.

2. Step-by-step recipes give you everything you need to get developing with Xamarin.

3. Full of useful tips and best practices on creating iOS applications.

Learning Xamarin Studio

ISBN: 978-1-78355-081-4   Paperback: 248 pages

Learn how to build high-performance native applications using the power of Xamarin Studio

1. Get a full introduction to the key features and components of the Xamarin 3 IDE and framework, including Xamarin.Forms and iOS visual designer.

2. Install, integrate and utilize Xamarin Studio with the tools required for building amazing cross-platform applications for iOS and Android.

3. Create, test, and deploy apps for your business and for the app store.

Please check **www.PacktPub.com** for information on our titles